YOU CAME BACK

From Iceland to Arnhem

ROBIN CARTWRIGHT

Ruth

All best wishes

Rob
18/01/2019

Rob Cartwright

Project management and editing by Cambridge Editorial Ltd www.camedit.com

Design by Paul Barrett Book Production www.pbbp.co.uk

Printed in Great Britain by Short Run Press
ISBN 978-1-5262-0372-4

CONTENTS

Acknowledgements

The writing of this book would have not been possible without the generosity of authors who had already recorded many of the events of the Second World War.

My thanks to John Benson who readily agreed to let me use material from his book *Saturday Night Soldiers*, the 4th Lincolns, the regiment my father fought with, and to Patrick Delaforce who wrote *The Polar Bears: Monty's Left Flank*, another invaluable source of information. Dennis Wilson agreed to the inclusion of his poem 'Aftermath'; likewise Janet Coward, the daughter of John Jarmain for 'At a War Grave'. Fiona Joseph was happy to let me use her work regarding the section on *Beatrice Cadbury – The Cadbury Heiress Who Gave Away Her Fortune*.

My thanks to my friends for their advice and for sharing their own stories: John Wakefield whose own book *Dad's War* was supportive in the early days of this project; Ian Fairlie for sharing his own father's experiences at Falaise Gap in Normandy, and Simon Partridge whose father fought in Norway. My old school friend Ralph Bennet sent me a moving description of the failed first attack on Arnhem, where his father was wounded and later imprisoned, and helped me with permission to use the cover illustration from the book *Old Whitwell*.

The Dutch department at University College London guided me to Scott Emblen-Jarrett for translation help; his assistance was invaluable. The staff at UCL Library, the Imperial War Museum and the British Library patiently showed me the IT skills needed to search out material.

In Holland my cousins Annelies, Liesbeth and Mattijs provided me with details about my Dutch family, the books about the liberation of Velp, the Rutgers family tree, and the story of the Yad Vashem award to the family. They put me in touch with Tami Shem-Tov, the author of *Letters from Nowhere* and Lieneke, the subject of that book, and her sister Rachel (van der Hoeden) in Israel. All were delighted to be contacted.

My thanks go to my family, my brothers and sisters who generously let me have so many of my parents' effects to use in preparing this book. Annemarie provided many copies of illustrations and photographs and Jane shared with me letters from my mother to her own family.

My children looked at the drafts of the work, making helpful and moving comments about their grandparents. My wife Wendy encouraged me to keep going with the words 'It has to be written for the next generation'.

References to many books are made in the text and these are listed in the bibliography.

If my parents had not kept so many records, photographs, scrapbooks and memorabilia of their time in the Second World War, the task would not have been possible. This book is dedicated to them and the many brave young soldiers and Dutch civilians who died during the years of that terrible war.

The story would not have been recognisable or readable without the guidance and encouragement of Rosalind Horton at Cambridge Editorial. Thanks also to Paul Barrett for his care in design and layout.

Preface

'You have come back, the British always do'

These were the words a lone Dutchmen said to a Second World War correspondent in the deserted, bomb-shattered ruins of a street in Arnhem following its liberation in April 1945. He was of course referring to the failed attempt to liberate the city in September 1944 – the ill-fated Operation Market Garden. If the Allied forces had not returned at the time they did, this story would never have been told. If my father had not been in the British forces that liberated Velp, near Arnhem, where he met my mother in the last month of the Second World War, this story would never had happened.

The re-emergence of newspaper articles, written by my mother in 1956 and serialised in a national newspaper, the *News Chronicle and Daily Dispatch*, rekindled the interest of all my family in the story of my parents. We thought about how they met, and the way we might talk about their story in the tributes to her at the time of her funeral. We had already talked about my father's account of his wartime experiences, which we described to everyone at his funeral six months earlier. We rediscovered some of the original photographs taken at the time my mother visited Arnhem, in 1956, to be reunited with old nursing friends and colleagues from her time in the hospital at Velp, the small town near Arnhem where she trained as a nurse during the war. It is from the series of articles in the *News Chronicle and Daily Despatch* that I started to base the structure of this story, as they were the source from which our family learned so much and appreciated what she had experienced. After my mother's death, we found more letters and papers that have helped fill in the story. It became clear there was more to tell about her life in Holland before she went to Velp to train as a nurse and my exploration of my father's time in the armed forces made me realise how briefly he had recorded the details of those years from 1940 to 1945.

Those articles, the photographs that my parents had kept, the written accounts they had been persuaded to record as well as letters to and from their own parents, made it possible to retell the fascinating tale of their experiences from 1940 to 1945 and the circumstances that led to their meeting in 1945. The surprise and sometimes astonishment of friends and family on hearing the story, in Holland as well as England, meant it had to be written and recorded for the next generation; to help them know about their grandparents, great-grandparents and family background.

All the family, in England and Holland, have contributed to this story. It has been a detective story in the process of collecting snippets of information, brief stories the family could recall, the gathering together of all the information discovered in published books and many sources found on the internet.

Introduction

My mother died in the early hours of the morning of 11 November 2012, just after her 89th birthday. Remembrance Day. A date appropriate to her life with my father, who had died some nine months earlier, at the age of 94. The events of the Second World War and their experiences in it shaped their future. My mother had spent the last two years of the war in Velp, a town near Arnhem, in Holland, while my father served in the British armed forces from 1940 to 1945. They met in Velp, at the time of the liberation of the city, in April 1945, in the last month of the Second World War in Europe at the time of the final liberation of Holland. At that time my father was one of a small group of British soldiers clearing houses in the ruined, heavily bombed city of Arnhem. Clearing houses was of course the inappropriate term used for the dangerous work soldiers had to do, moving swiftly from house to house across rubble to search out any remaining occupying German forces. The city had been appallingly damaged, due initially to the action the previous September, the failed Operation Market Garden, and recent heavy Allied forces bombing, in preparation for the assault on Arnhem and the cities on the north side of the Rhine. The date my parents met was told to me as 5 April 1945 but other sources indicate it must have been nearer the 15th. My father and his comrades had found a piano, remarkably intact, in a ruined house in Velp. He started to play. By chance, a small group of nurses from the nearby hospital had been allowed out into the streets. They heard the music he was playing, 'Begin the Beguine', a popular song at the time. Although originally a term used to describe a Christian religious order, the Beguine was a word that came to be used in the Caribbean to mean a white woman, and later developed to describe a dance, similar to a slow rhumba, its popularity increasing in Europe after Cole Porter composed his song 'Begin the Beguine'. The group of nurses sought out the source of the music, and found the soldiers. Perhaps it was love at first sight, on the part of my mother and father. Suitably impressed, the nurses invited the pianist and his comrades to 'help' at a small celebration party that had been planned in the hospital, the fighting in the area finally finished and the area liberated. The young pianist had the company of my mother most of the evening of the party and they were able to continue seeing each other. The romance flourished, and their life together as a couple began.

This story, then, is a memoir of my parents of the time they spent in the years of the Second World War before they met and fell in love, a story of one happy outcome from the horrors of that particular war, a story that merits telling. The impetus finally to write something that would bring together the varied tales and small references they had passed on to us arose as a result of the death of both my parents within the same year, 2012.

As a family we all knew the tale of how our parents met and the romance that followed at the very end of the Second World War, but I always knew there was much they had both left unsaid about what they had been through in those five years. One reason for convincing me it was worthwhile spending a long time writing this memoir was provided by my sister Annemarie. Not long after mother's death and funeral, she was at school teaching and her class had been asked to contribute to a poster display of inspirational people. Our mother was in her mind and she came up with the idea of our mother, whose own story had been part of a recent Second World War exhibition at Hereford Cathedral, featured in the local paper, the *Hereford Times*. My sister had found her an inspirational person and the suggestion went down very well with the children in her class. Her colleagues, other teachers, were not aware of the background of someone they had known for years, living in Leominster, the town in the county of Hereford where my parents spent their final years. When our mother died, I contacted our relatives in Holland, including my mother's cousin Nieske, to let her know. Nieske is only a little older than me and I had last met her about two years earlier in London, with my other sister, Jane, although I had of course seen her as a girl on family visits, both in Holland and England. She replied to me, beginning:

Dear Robin
My condolences for your mother. Who passed by. My English is terrible, but I hope you understand me. How is your father? I regret that in the last 2–3 years I never heart anything. [sic]

She concluded:

I thank you that you informed me. Your mother was a woman, for me, who understood everything, because also she was married, with a stranger. I'm not able, to explain to you what I feel now and how important your mother was for me.

My mother had been able to talk about her wartime experiences in the hospital in Velp, a suburb of Arnhem in Holland, where she trained as a nurse. Indeed at times there was a sense of excitement in the stories she relayed to us, as well as the tension and fear that was often present and as we will see had her story in part recorded as a series of articles in a national newspaper in early 1956 so that we were more familiar with it. Underneath that ability to recount her experiences, though, there was a deep trauma. I was a young boy aged nine years old in 1956 when the Suez Crisis arose. I am not able to say how realistic the prospect of war was, but the feeling or threat was enough to make my mother support emigration to Australia, to Adelaide (which I think was thought to be 'more English'), under the assisted passage scheme. The impending arrival of my youngest sister Jane meant this plan was taken no further. The facts may not be entirely correct but the emotions present to examine such a drastic move must have been very powerful.

My father was always reluctant to talk about what had happened during his time in war – a common experience of men returning from conflict and battle. The affection that my Dutch relatives felt for him was clear, but I had not realised how much he, and his comrades, were honoured by the Dutch family and the people they had liberated from the terror of the Nazi occupation.

When we let our Dutch cousins know of his death, we were moved by their response and the efforts they made to travel to his funeral, a reflection not only of their affection for him but of the respect the Dutch civilians still have for their liberators. Evert, the oldest son of my mother's brother Dick, let me know in his correspondence of his travel plans, saying that of course:

he was coming to the funeral, age 94, an old soldiers never dies [sic]

After some persuasion from my sister Annemarie, my father wrote down an account of his wartime experiences, for up to this point we knew only what he had told us in short conversations and always after prompting, never volunteered by him. He had talked about his time in Iceland and how despite the freezing temperatures he had never had a cold. How he had boxed when in the army, describing the ring as 'a lonely place' and of course the music, including the chance to play in a band with musicians whom in their civilian life might have been professionals. Only on one occasion did he tell me about the first fighting action in which he was involved and the horrendous outcome, when his closest friend at the time was killed. In his account, he omitted much of the most traumatic, preferring to get to the end of the story, and his time in Holland at the end of the war. It has become apparent to me, at the time of writing this, and having just attended a moving Remembrance Day service, that the reason he never joined the British Legion, or took part in the annual Remembrance Day parades and services, was that it was possibly too painful for him. Many years later, after his retirement from the teaching profession, he suffered a long period of clinical anxiety, which I am sure was linked to his wartime experiences and although it did not prevent him from having a full productive retirement, was a tiresome state to cope with. He began his account of his wartime experiences with these words:

> You asked me to write down some memories of my experiences in the Second World War. This is something I have never done, and may even have avoided, BUT SINCE YOU ATTACH SOME IMPORTANCE TO IT I have tried putting some memories together. At times in Normandy it was difficult to remember where you were, OR EVEN WHY, so they are just memories. (My capitals.)

Without those memories and his account, it would have been difficult to write this story. His full story appears at the end of this book as Appendix 1.

CHAPTER ONE

Whitwell, Derbyshire 1918–40

My father's early life

My father was born in Whitwell, a small village in North East Derbyshire, in 1917. My grandparents, Sid and Annie, arrived in Whitwell in 1913, the first family of that name in the village. They were known to us all as Opa and Oma Cartwright, those being the Dutch names for grandparents. They had come from the 'Black Country' (the West Midlands) in order to establish themselves in secure employment in the new colliery – 'the Pit' – which had been opened just after the turn of the century. The reason for the move was that the seams of coal in the collieries in the West Midlands were (relatively!) easy to mine for coal but were now becoming worked out. The development of the new coalfield in North East Derbyshire had started at the turn of the century and promised a more secure future. 'Opa Cartwright', my grandfather, came first to Derbyshire to look for employment and somewhere to live. He managed to secure both and returned to Brierley Hill in the West Midlands to marry a young Annie Waldron, my grandmother. All the family, that is Sid and his new wife, his three younger sisters and his parents packed up their belongings, left Staffordshire, and headed for Whitwell, making the journey by long boat on the canals. This journey would have taken them from Dudley through the West Midlands Canal system along the River Trent basin to join the canal

My father, aged two.

system leading through Worksop, where I assume the family disembarked, to reach their new home. The change to diesel engines to power the boats was becoming more widespread and so I believe the trip would therefore not have been by the old way, being towed by a horse on the canal towpath. My great-grandparents, Tom and Celia, were head of the family, and relocated to Whitwell on the same journey, but we can only guess at his age and it is not clear whether Tom senior worked in the coalmines. We must assume they all lived together, but not at the small terraced house with the shop that I remember in Welbeck Street.

The Cartwrights were a close-knit family, and my grandfather's three sisters – Ivy, Dolly and Lily – took 'Annie' his new wife, under their wing, as she had left all her family behind in the Midlands. These three sisters, my great-aunts, all married local men and settled in the village, taking the names of Bell, Owens and Limb, very familiar to me and I have very clear memories of them all. The Bell family lived a few doors away from where my mother and father lived in their first family home together, in Bakestone Moor on the outskirts of Whitwell; the Limbs lived further along the crescent in the same council housing development and the Owens opposite the small terraced house in Welbeck Street where my father grew up.

Research done by my uncle looked at the family tree as far back as the early 1800s. It shows my father was descended from a very humble background. A look at the entries on the various documents that he copied for his research makes me think of how we live now and what we take for granted in our education, ambitions and lifestyle. One thing I can remember my father telling me is that my grandmother's schooling stopped age 13 and she entered domestic service, initially as a maid with responsibility for cleaning and blacking all the fireplaces at the home where she was employed. Copies of the marriage certificates show occupations of the family such as nailmaker and spade maker, and the documented entries on the certificates often reads 'the mark X of the bride or groom'. The 1891 census shows that my father's great-grandparents were alive and living in Quarry Bank near Dudley in the West Midlands and his great-grandfather's occupation was given as toolmaker and cordwainer (a shoemaker).

My father's full name was Percy Albert Cartwright, the middle of three children and often referred to as 'our Butt' by the family (an abbreviation of his middle name). He was a bright intelligent boy who started his education in the local village school, from which he won a rare scholarship to The Brunts School in Mansfield, just over the county border in Nottinghamshire. It was then a grammar school, now a comprehensive, a recent alumna being Rebecca Adlington, the swimmer and Olympic gold medallist.

Had the scholarship not been possible, he would have followed his father and uncles into the coalmines, as indeed his younger brother Barry did, until 'rescued' and persuaded to train as a teacher. Barry completed a P.E. teaching diploma in Exeter and married 'Aunty Di'. Barry was the uncle I mentioned earlier who undertook a lot of research into the details recounted above which, in those days before the internet, required actual visits to the registration offices of the counties in which the family lived, usually taking two to three days to complete the searches. Barry, although much younger than my father, predeceased him, his last years being spent in a nursing home as a result of his disabling Parkinson's disease.

My father had an older sister, Cissy. She had a leg amputated as a result of osteomyelitis contracted in childhood, and always used a crutch having never had a prosthesis fitted. She married Jack Owens, another miner, but never had children and remained in the village of Whitwell all her life, until her death in 1980. My father kept some of his school reports and records; they show he was good at games, particularly football, and that he took English, history and French at higher certificate in the sixth form. I had not realised this and I wondered why more use had not been made of this during his time in the forces in France. I know that, initially, after being called up to join the armed forces, he had been part of the education corps, before joining the mortar platoon.

His mother Annie, Oma Cartwright as we knew her, was a tough character who at one point before and during the war years, when they lived in Welbeck Road, ran a local corner shop. The Whitwell History Society records:

> It is doubtful if shopping in Supermarkets today will leave fascinating memories such as those we have of the shops in Whitwell. They each had their own individuality – Cartwright's, handy to the rec. [sic] with groceries and sweets.

Remarkably, after the war she was able to buy her own house, Bridge House, on Station Road near the colliery and this is the house I remembered them living in when I was a child. Her husband Sid, my grandfather, continued to work in the mine until he retired, sadly to die soon after, in 1966, of renal cancer. He was a 'character'. My sister Annemarie recalls staying with our grandparents in the school holidays and listening to an early morning conversation coming up the stairs: 'Sid, Sid, come on, get up I can hear all the men whistling and talking on the way to work.' The reply came 'Aye, I can't hear any women's voices there.'

I have clear recollections of stays there, with my grandparents, the traditional Sunday lunch, with bicarbonate of soda in the greens, tasting the 'spuds' with Opa Cartwright to see if they were ready, and all the cooking done on the coal-fuelled kitchen range. This on Sundays was followed by a late tea – if possible tinned (red) salmon, beetroot and pickles. No need for supper! On a Saturday night, after a trip to the Miners' Welfare club on Hanger Hill, Opa Cartwright loved to hear a rendition of 'Danny Boy', the well-known Irish lament, played on the violin by my father. Music had always been a big feature of my father's life, with violin lessons and playing as a youngster, but as he was to tell me, no formal piano lessons, which makes his musical skills even more remarkable. After Sid died, Oma Cartwright moved to sheltered accommodation in the village, selling Bridge House to Barbara Bell, her niece. Eventually Oma had to move, to live with my parents in Herefordshire before finally going into the Waverley Care Home in Leominster, where she died in 1986.

The love and affection my father had for his family will be seen later in this story, a moving account he wrote of his feelings as the final fighting finished for him in Holland. After my parents married in 1946 they lived with the family in Welbeck Street, staying for some nine months after I was born, until they were able to rent a small flat in a farmhouse at Pebley, a tiny hamlet near Whitwell.

My father's upbringing shaped a great deal of his views and outlook on life. He told us stories of the general strike of 1926, when he would have been eight years old, describing the hunger and privation and bitter struggles of that time. During his childhood, the 'pit', as the colliery was always known, was the place most of the men in the village worked and the coalmining industry shaped the development of the village at that time. The mine was still fully worked when I was a boy in Franklin Crescent, in Bakestone Moor, the address of my parents' first independent family home. The pit was one of five opened by the Shireoaks Colliery Company.

In 1890 the sixth Duke of Portland cut and lifted the first sod on the site of the new Whitwell Colliery and the sinking of No. 1 shaft began. Up to that point, at the turn of the century, Whitwell had been a typical rural village, and by the 1930s the coalmine was still the only major employer.

One event that changed the lives of the miners was the building of the pithead baths in 1935, the first sod being cut again by the sixth Duke of Portland on 6 June, using the same silver spade presented to him after the cutting of the first sod to open the pit 45 years earlier. Prior to this, the men would return to their home in their pit clothes, and washing was usually done in a large tub in the front room, few homes having a bathroom. The pit also started to provide gas for supply to the houses in the village and eventually electric lighting was supplied by a generator situated at the pit. The cost I note was recorded as nine old pence, 9d, a week in the summer and 18d a week during the winter.

A detailed story of the Whitwell Colliery has been written by the Whitwell local history group, right thorough to the 1980s. The end of this era, of a village dominated by the mining industry, was controversial and bitter. The miners' strike of 1984–85 led to deep divisions in the community, creating family rifts, some never healed, as the few miners who initially crossed the picket lines were joined by a further trickle, forced on them by increasing hardship and misery. My father never liked Arthur Scargill, the left-wing NUM leader whose confrontational manner increased the unforgivable actions of the Thatcher government. He realised the industry had to change, but abhorred the way it was forced to do so. The last worker finished in July 1987 and the process of demolition and filling in the shafts began. The landscape was altered, but the 96 years of colliery working had left an indelible influence on the life of the parish.

The Portland family were very much a part of local history, as seen by the fact that the sixth Duke performed the ceremonial opening of the colliery at Whitwell. They were hereditary landowners in the area. When I became aware of the odd story of the fifth Duke of Portland, the previous heir to the title, my father confirmed that indeed 'everyone in the village knew about him and his odd ways'. The Duke, William John Cavendish-Bentinck-Scott, succeeded to the title in 1854. He was a bizarre eccentric Victorian aristocrat who had the wealth to construct a labyrinth of tunnels around his home, Welbeck Abbey, in order that he could move around the estate either unseen by his staff, or upon his instruction be ignored if seen. He increasingly only ventured out at night, and took to having his food delivered to his rooms on heated trolleys. By the time of his death in December 1870 only the rooms he inhabited in the vast house were habitable. *The Underground Man*, by Mick Jackson, a fascinating read, is a fictionalised account of the Duke and his mental illness, a delusional paranoid state of mind. It is also very descriptive of detail of the social inequalities of the time, although the Duke took an interest in his tenants' welfare and was known as 'the people's friend'. Another reference to him is made by Bill Bryson in his *Notes from a Small Island*, when Bryson visits Clumber Park, part of the estate, and investigates the stories he has heard of the Duke.

The images of the village of those days have been delightfully captured by the sketches and paintings as a collection in *Old Whitwell*, a book by James Cross, who ran the village barber shop and was a talented watercolour artist. By coincidence, I was collecting my grandson from the home of a friend of my daughter Georgina, when I recognised a painting on the hallway wall, instantly recognisable as the Church of St Lawrence, by Jim Cross. We exchanged astonished reminiscences and it transpired that her uncle was Ralph, a schoolboy friend of mine. Ralph's own father, well known to our family, had been a Red Beret in the Paratroops and wounded at Arnhem at the time of the first battle of Arnhem. My mother helped translate his POW records for the local medical practice, but more of that later.

After leaving school my father went to train as a teacher in the West Midlands, at Dudley College of Education, lodging with his Uncle Jim and Aunt Nellie in Wolverhampton, from where he cycled daily to the college. I never knew why he chose there, although it was the area my grandparents originally came from, but perhaps it was simply because accommodation could not be found for him nearer the college. He talked with great affection

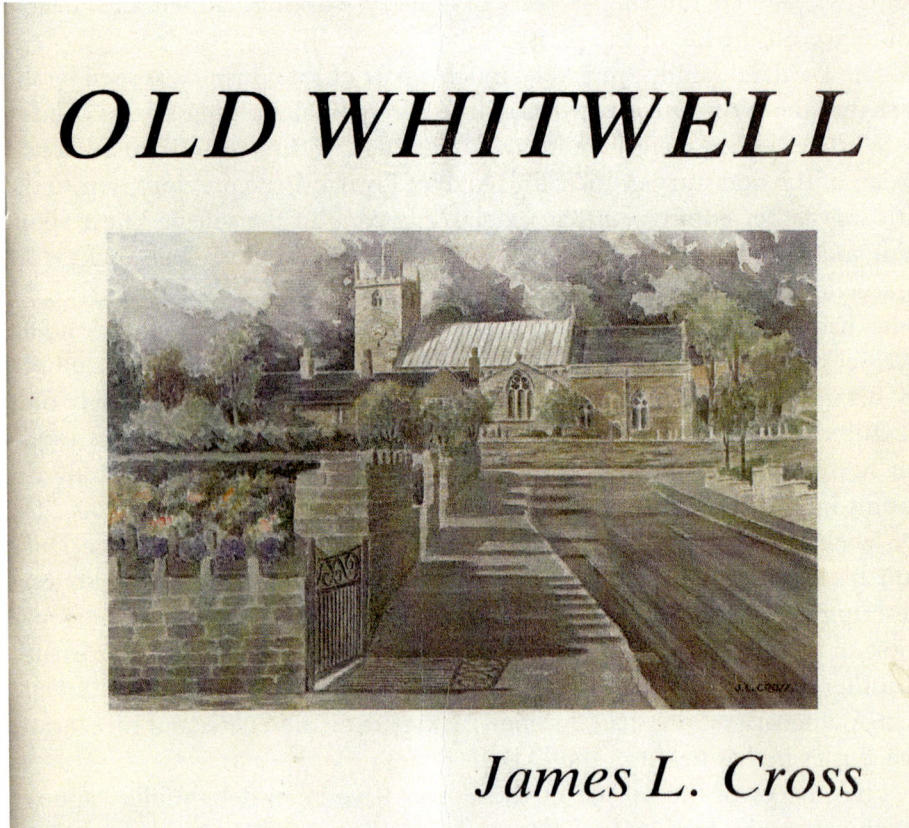

The Church of St Lawrence, Whitwell.

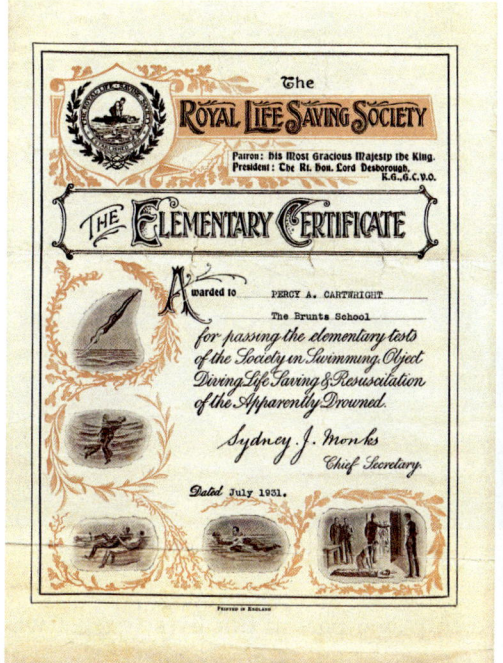

My father was a very competent swimmer.

With Jim and Nellie at the races.

A promising footballer – my father is back row, third from right.

With friends at Dudley College.

about Nellie and Jim who continued to play a part in our lives when I was a child as we stayed for holidays at their retirement bungalow near the small town of Kinver, in Worcestershire. A photograph taken years later shows my father with Nellie and Jim at the races.

At college, playing football was my father's main sport and he was proud to relate to me that the college team had played against the reserve team of West Bromwich Albion, who were then a football league first division side. The onset of war stole his best footballing years; we know he had been 'chased' by both West Bromwich Albion and Bury FC to join them so who knows what might have happened had one of them succeeded in signing him on to their books.

After completing his training, he moved back to Derbyshire, and took an appointment as an assistant master at Welbeck College, before being appointed in 1939 to a post at Shirebrooke, a nearby village, to begin what he hoped would be a career in the teaching profession.

However, the political situation in Europe moved from aggression and rhetoric to invasion; war was imminent and Britain declared war on Germany in 1939. By 1940 his first teaching appointment was over, and life was to change for ever, as it had begun to do for a girl across the north sea in Holland.

CHAPTER TWO

Vriezenveen, Holland 1923–40

My mother's early life

My mother was born in Vriezenveen, a village in a rural farming community in the north east of the Netherlands, near the German border. Life was very different in the village back then; most farmers still wore wooden clogs (called 'klompen') for outdoor work. Oddly enough, Vriezenveen is the last or only site in the Netherlands for a pre-positioned NATO combat unit, manned by a few military personnel and Dutch civilians.

There were six children in the family, my mother being the third. Doortje and Gerrie were her elder sisters, followed by Nanny and Rikje. Dick, her only brother, was nearly the same age as she was. Their father, Evert Rutgers, was a veterinary surgeon and their mother was named Hendrika (née Van Oene).

Considerable research into the family tree was done by my Aunt Rikje in Holland and this has been continued by my cousin Liesbeth and her husband Youri. My mother wrote a short note about her family ancestors, telling us of the ancestry on her mother's side of the family. It begins as follows:

My grandmother's side of the family were descended from the Huguenots fleeing persecution in France, following the St Bartholomew's Day Massacre, 1572, the wave of Roman Catholic mob violence against the Huguenots, the French Calvinist

My mother with the family's pet dog.

Protestants. The family name of my great-grandmother was 'Le Cointre', and the family name can be traced back to 1795. Tracing through the descendants to 1859, we can see the names of Anthony Le Cointre, an Apothecary ('Chymist') and Hendrik, a Doctor and Gynaecologist in Zeeland. In the register of family names of the Pas de Calais, the name Le Cointre is common, often mentioned in Boulogne. The meaning of the name Le Cointre can be linked to the old French 'cointe', itself coming from the Latin 'cognitus', which means wise and experienced, a family name to be proud of.

This was a very different family background from my father's and might help explain my mother's interest in and wish to pursue a medical career.

Our great-great grandmother was Hendrika Marie Le Cointre, born in 1837. The family had settled in Zeeland, a province in southern Holland. Her first name has been passed through the generations; my cousin has the Dutch version 'Henrietta'. After marriage to a Dirk de Oude in Goes, she had a son, also called Dirk, born in 1862. Dirk junior married Theodora Winkelman, my great-grandmother, in 1891. This was 'little Oma' as we knew her. She would have seen me as a baby in Holland on a visit back by my mother and father, the proud new parents.

'Little Oma' with the author, Holland, 1947.

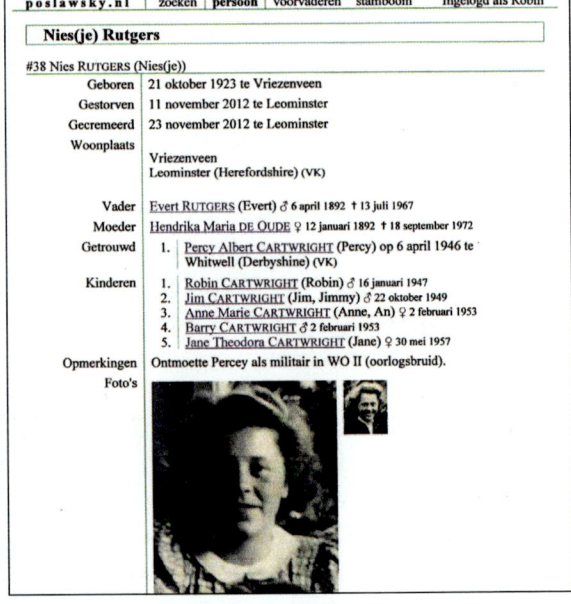

Taken from the Rutgers' family tree.

The newly wedded couple, 'Little Oma Winkleman' and Dirk then moved to and settled in Zaltbommel, in the province of Gelderland in the south of Holland. There she gave birth to a daughter, Hendrika Marie, who would eventually marry Evert Rutgers, my grandfather (Opa Holland), a young man from the same town and whom she first met at school. I was very touched to read the obituary of Evert Rutgers, Opa Holland, translated by Youri, the husband of my cousin in Holland. The second paragraph reads as follows:

Opa and Oma Holland on their wedding day.

Rutgers Evert was born in Zaltbommel on April 5th 1892. He went to kindergarten, primary school and secondary school. Why list the kindergarten here? Because there is a photograph of a class of that school, in which a little boy stands next to a little girl holding hands. That girl, Riek De Oude, would later become his wife in Zaltbommel in 1917 and they would go through life together as a couple.

We would all love to trace that photograph.

The origins of my grandfather's side of the family are illustrated by a photograph familiar to all the Rutgers – the family windmill near Zaltbommel. It was operated by our great-grandfather's brother Arnoldus W. Rutgers (1855–1943), before it burned down. Pieces of it, such as the barge-board,

My Dutch grandparents after the war.

My Dutch grandparents when we met up in 1966.

The Rutgers family windmill.

The Windmill of Rutger

Uncle Reyer (my father's brother)
his 2 children Gerda & Gerrit and
their cousin Piet.
Aunt Corrie (my father's sister,
unmarried) and more cousins:
Arnold and Mies.
The mill was run by my
grandfather Arnold W. Rutgers
(1855-1943) until it
burned down in
There are still pieces of it
(large boards etc.) in the museum

in Zalt-Bommel, at the
river Waal in the southern
Netherlands. It stood on
a bank (wal in Dutch)
surrounding that part of the
town adjoining the river.
(You can see the mast of the
ship in the back ground).
To this day that road is
called: Molen wal
(or Mill-bank)

are in the museum in Zaltbommel. It stood on a bank ('wal' in Dutch) on the side of the River Waal, a river which, nearly a century later, played a significant part in this story. In the photograph we can see the mast of a ship in the background, and in the foreground some of the family. My mother identified these as her uncle Reyer, her cousins Gerda and Gerrit and Corrie, the older lady, her unmarried aunt.

Life would seem to have been comfortable for the Rutgers family in the 1930s. I am told my grandfather was a very good veterinary surgeon, but expensive! If farmers could not pay money, then food was always left and accepted. He was a well-educated man, both speaking and writing fluent English. My memories of him are hazy, but I know I never saw him dressed other than in a suit, invariably smoking a cigar or cigarette. On one occasion he painstakingly explained to me the rules of 'Sjoelbak', the popular indoor board game we call Dutch Shuffleboard. When I told him I had started to study French at school he apologised ruefully, sad that he had lost, or forgotten, all his French. The Rutgers family lived in a substantial house, with the type of help a middle-class family would have had then. Mother was a good student, gifted at languages, and a keen swimmer, as we can see from her swimming certificate.

She had hoped to study medicine at university, but the outbreak of the Second World War prevented this happening. She was 16 years old at the

My mother obtained her swimming diploma in 1936, five years after my father obtained his life saving certificate from the Brunts School in England.

time of the invasion and occupation of Holland by Germany, and so going to medical school was not possible. She continued to live with the family in Vriezenveen until 1942 where she began her nursing training the following year, the plans to read medicine no longer being possible. A photograph, taken at or near their home in Vriezenveen, shows a happy bunch of children. Doortje, the eldest, is on the right of the photograph. She never married or had children and was born with a chromosome abnormality (Turner's Syndrome). She was devoted to her parents, and was herself looked after fondly in later life by the family. Gerrie, the next daughter, was to leave home first, and marry Sieb, also a veterinary surgeon, which

The family with their dog in Vriezenveen.

delighted Opa Holland. Dick is the tall young boy, who would later become active in the Dutch resistance movement in the war. Rikje, whom we also see later in a photograph with my mother and 'cousin Francine', stands between Gerrie and Dick, while my mother is bottom left with Nannie the youngest in between, all standing behind the family pet. Nannie was with her parents throughout the war, is now elderly and widowed and we were moved by the effort made to enable her to make the trip across to England to attend the funeral of her older sister, my mother, in 2012.

My mother – always a keen swimmer – loved to swim in the sea at Scheveningen and in the canals.

She talked about her time in the Girl Guides and in later life organised exchange trips to Holland for the movement. She welcomed guides to the small town of Leominster where my parents settled, and in fact was away at a guide camp when the comfortable and warm family life of the Rutgers was violently interrupted on 10 May 1940 when the defences of Holland and Belgium were smashed open. The German invasion had begun, with troops pouring in from the border so close to the Rutgers family.

Meanwhile, four months before that, back in England, a young man's career was halted. My father had been called up to join the Allied forces.

CHAPTER THREE

Iceland, May 1940– September 1942

My father's time in the army starts

I was in my first teaching post in Shirebrook, eight miles from Whitwell, when I was called up in January 1940. Lofty Burgin from Worksop was in the same batch and we were still together at the end of the war. We trained at Lincoln Barracks in May that year and then went to Hawick in Scotland to join the 4th Lincolns.

The 4th Lincolns were the 4th battalion of the Lincolnshire Regiment, known as the 'Terriers' and sometimes jokingly as the 'Saturday Night Soldiers'. They were formed from the voluntary 'back-up reserve' for the British Army when there was no conscription in peacetime. Almost every town in England had such a force. The 4th battalion of the Lincolnshire Regiment was perhaps different from most, in that due to the size of the county and relatively sparse population, the men could be drawn from places as far apart as 40 miles. This would explain why, although living in Derbyshire, when my father was called up this was the unit he joined. The history of the actions and engagements of the 4th Lincolns has been meticulously recorded in the book *Saturday Night Soldiers*, written by John Benson, himself a Lincolnshire man. From this I have been able to obtain much information to enable me to plot the progress

Called up.

of my father and his mortar platoon in 'D' company from Iceland, across France and Belgium and finally to Holland.

The 4th Lincolns had arrived at Stobs Camp near Hawick in Scotland on Thursday 9 May. On Tuesday 18 June they were moved to Dunkeld and five days later by rail to the Clyde to board the liner HMS *Andes* and set sail for Iceland.

In his account of his wartime experiences my father wrote:

On the 24th June we sailed to Iceland. Looking back that was a good place to be! By autumn we were in Nissen huts. As it's practically in the Arctic Circle it's dark for virtually 24 hours in December, and the reverse in June.

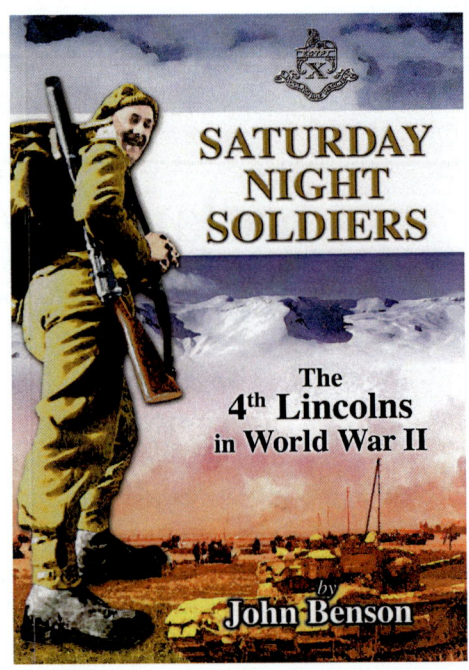

My father was one of the Saturday Night Soldiers.

The Northern lights were fascinating, and it was very healthy – I never had a cold there. Akureyri was a town of 6,500 people. It had a cinema and an OUTDOOR pool. Training was all the year round. I remember being lost and walking over a glacier and camping out in February. I played a lot of football and played violin with the Northern Lights Dance Band, who actually broadcast from Reykjavik.

After the German conquest of Denmark and the invasion of Norway, the spotlight had turned upon Iceland and its strategic position in the path of the North Atlantic sea lanes. Iceland had by agreement with Denmark in 1918 become a separate state under the Danish crown, with control of its own affairs excepting international relations. It was a remote, barren, volcanic realm with little development and, at the time, in 1940, had a population of only 140,000. It was recognised, however, to have a strategic position along the North Atlantic sea lanes and assumed a new importance to British strategic thinking. German interest in Iceland had continued to grow, a suspicious number of 'anthropology teams' from Germany had arrived to survey the island and Lufthansa attempted unsuccessfully to establish an airline service, while commercial trade also increased dramatically. The Foreign Office

My father is middle row, kneeling, to the left of Colin Hartley, who would become his best man.

The camp and resting outside the 'accommodation' in Iceland, and recovering from a swim.

determined there was no chance of a negotiated agreement to allow plans for a British presence on the island and the war cabinet of Prime Minister Winston Churchill decided to land first and negotiate later as Iceland continued to confirm its neutrality. In early May before the 4th Lincolns arrived, the Royal Marines entered Reykjavik, the capital, secured key locations, seized the German consulate and took German residents into custody. At exactly that time, on 10 May, the German offensive against France and the Low Countries started. The Icelandic government then tacitly accepted the British occupation and importantly it was supported by the USA, although it was not until 16 August 1941 that Winston Churchill visited the island; the only photograph easily located shows him reviewing a force of marines from the USA.

The troop transport ship HMS *Andes*, with the 4th Lincolns aboard, had an unpleasant stormy journey from the Clyde estuary in Scotland. They landed on the afternoon of 28 June at Iceland's most northern port, Akureyri, giving the Lincolns an immediate experience of the phenomenon of the midnight sun. The 4th Lincolns had been allocated the responsibility of guarding the north-eastern coastline, based around Akureyri.

The Icelandic population as a whole were not all enthusiastic about the presence of the British, and my father never really talked to us about them. The impression seemed to be that the Icelanders gradually became a little more friendly, efforts were made to use their skills and provide some employment, but it must have been a shock for the troops to see the conditions that the local population lived in, often primitive shacks made of sods of earth. Fish was of course plentiful, but no fruit and virtually no vegetables were grown, so the men had to rely heavily on tinned imported food. The purpose of the training that the division undertook was to have troops ready, trained in winter warfare conditions, in the event of an invasion of Norway by the German forces. My father told me of training with long trips in the snow, once getting lost on a glacier and the experiences of sleeping out in tents on the ice. Ski platoon training was done under the guidance of Norwegian instructors and survival training in two-man tents with weapons, rations and a stove. With temperatures that would drop as low as minus 40 degrees by December it was with great relief that the Nissen huts arrived before the winter. My father told me he would never camp again, after this experience, but he did relent in later years, accompanying the Derbyshire Schools to camp at Red Wharf Bay on the island of Anglesey, just off the coast of Wales.

The 49th Division, an infantry division of the British Army, by now had its own insignia, a polar bear, looking for all it was worth like an advertisement for Fox's Glacier Mints It was kept through the whole campaign. It

The orchestra performed to a high standard. My father is far left, with violin. We can see the programme for the concert given by the orchestra in January 1942, and in the orchestra list of three violins, Pte P. A. Cartwright is named.

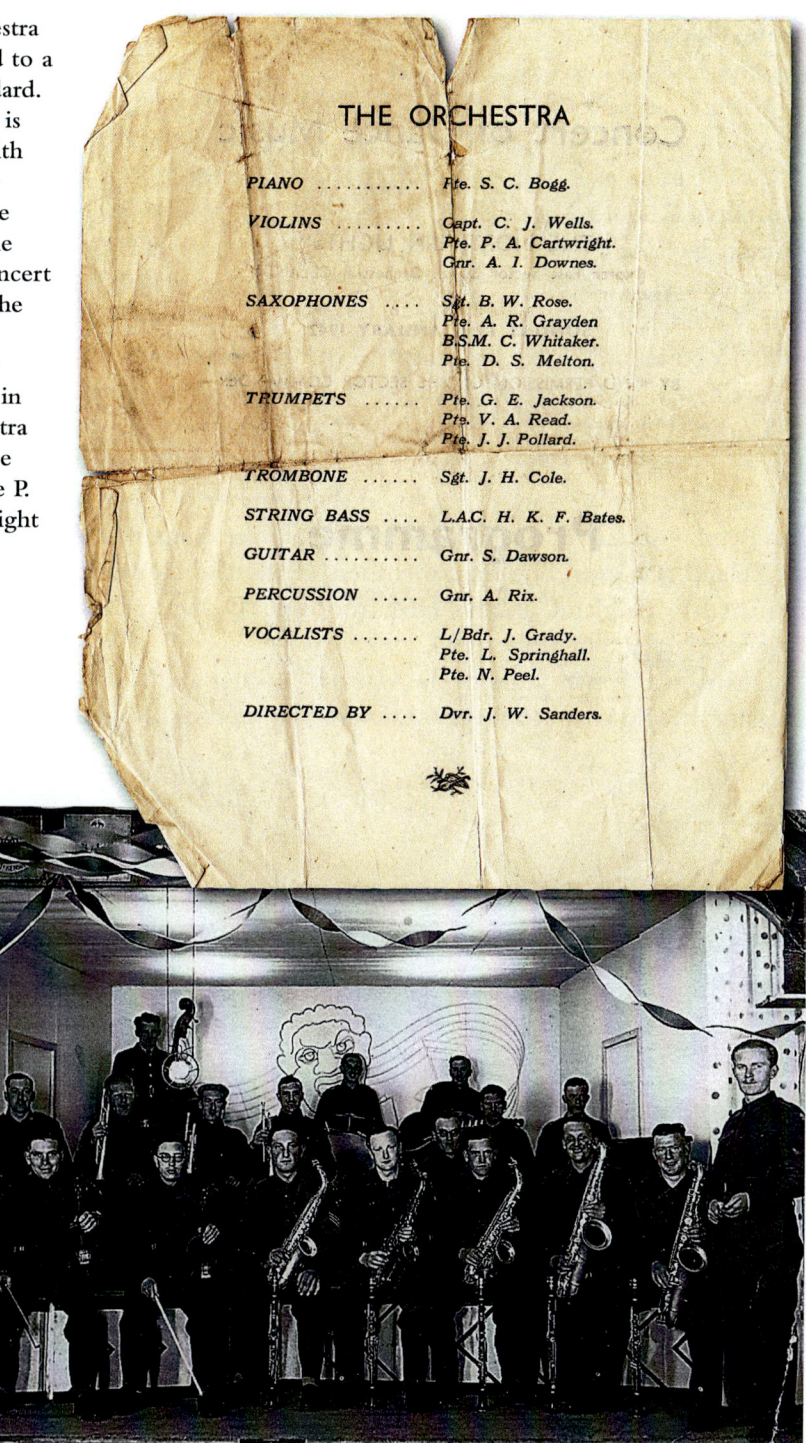

THE ORCHESTRA

PIANO	Pte. S. C. Bogg.
VIOLINS	Capt. C. J. Wells.
	Pte. P. A. Cartwright.
	Gnr. A. I. Downes.
SAXOPHONES	Sgt. B. W. Rose.
	Pte. A. R. Grayden
	B.S.M. C. Whitaker.
	Pte. D. S. Melton.
TRUMPETS	Pte. G. E. Jackson.
	Pte. V. A. Read.
	Pte. J. J. Pollard.
TROMBONE	Sgt. J. H. Cole.
STRING BASS	L.A.C. H. K. F. Bates.
GUITAR	Gnr. S. Dawson.
PERCUSSION	Gnr. A. Rix.
VOCALISTS	L/Bdr. J. Grady.
	Pte. L. Springhall.
	Pte. N. Peel.
DIRECTED BY	Dvr. J. W. Sanders.

seemed not to matter that there were no polar bears in Iceland, only ponies, rats and a few white foxes.

A more pleasant diversion from the training was being able to play in the NLO, the Northern Lights Orchestra, created from the troops on the base.

Morale must have been low during the long winter months, and there was a minimal Red Cross presence, as recorded in a book *They Sent me to Iceland* written by Jane Goodell who records filling many roles – cook, secretary, nurse and organiser of dances and entertainment in the oft forgotten outpost.

It would not be long before the British forces were reinforced by US military personnel. After the entry of the USA into the Second World War following the attack by the Japanese airforce on Pearl Harbor in December 1941, the occupation of Iceland, which had already begun to assume importance in American planning, was taken over by USA troops, and the withdrawal of British personnel began. In the summer of 1942 most of the units had been withdrawn as it finally seemed that the danger of German invasion of Iceland was over. The final members of the battalion of the 4th Lincolns returned to England on the HM troopship *Duchess of Bedford*, landing in Liverpool on 9 September 1942.

During those two years of the war my mother and the Rutgers family in Holland had to adapt to a very different way of life.

CHAPTER FOUR

Holland, May 1940

Invasion

Holland, along with the Scandinavian countries, had contrived to remain neutral in the First World War. It was hoped, as the intentions of Hitler's Germany became clear, that Holland could remain neutral again. During the winter of 1939–40 the Dutch parliament had tried to take no action that might provoke the German high command in the hope of remaining neutral. But to no avail. At dawn on 10 May 1940, the day after my father arrived in Scotland to prepare for departure to Iceland, the German assault on Holland, Belgium and France began. There was brief resistance, with some successful Dutch fighting in the area surrounding The Hague and the Ijsselmeer Dam, leading to an escalation of the German attacks, but the inevitable was soon to happen. After the centre of Rotterdam was heavily bombed on 15 May, the Dutch Army was ordered to capitulate in order to avoid the threat of further destruction. This was then the five-day war, and the fact that there was resistance and fighting, with a relatively high number of German casualties

Rotterdam was bombed into submission.

EVENING STANDARD, May 10, 1940

LATE SPECIAL

This is
the Gin
Gordon's
Stands
Supreme

Evening Standard

Amusements 10
Radio 10

BLACK-OUT 9.5 pm, 4.47 am.
MOON Rose 7.37 am; Sets 11.24 pm.

No. 36,093   LONDON, FRIDAY, MAY 10, 1940   ONE PENNY

NAZIS INVADE HOLLAND, BELGIUM, LUXEMBURG: MANY AIRPORTS BOMBED
Allies Answer Call for Aid: R.A.F. Planes are in Action

HITLER HAS INVADED HOLLAND, BELGIUM AND LUXEMBURG. HIS PARACHUTE TROOPS ARE LANDING AT SCORES OF POINTS AND MANY AIRPORTS ARE BEING BOMBED.

THE DUTCH HAVE OPENED THEIR FLOOD-GATES AND CLAIM TO HAVE BROUGHT DOWN A DOZEN BOMBERS.

It was confirmed in official quarters in London shortly after 8 a.m. to-day that appeals for assistance have been received from both the Belgian and Dutch Governments, and that these Governments have been told that H.M. Government will, of course, render all the help they can.

Every airport in Belgium has been attacked by Nazi airplanes, it is announced in Brussels.

BRUSSELS IS BEING "BOMBARDED TERRIFICALLY," SAYS A NEW YORK MESSAGE.

A Zurich report states that casualties in the first raid over Brussels amounted to 400 dead and wounded.

Lyons Airport Bombed

Other reports say that Antwerp and the airport at Lyons (France) have been bombed.

THE BELGIAN ARMY IS RESISTING THE GERMAN INVASION, IT IS OFFICIALLY ANNOUNCED IN PARIS. GENERAL MOBILISATION HAS BEEN PROCLAIMED.

BRUSSELS RADIO ANNOUNCE THAT ALLIED TROOPS ARE ON THE WAY TO BELGIUM'S AID.

French, Belgian and British airplanes have been sighted over Holland, states an official Dutch announcement.

"These airplanes," it was added, "belong to our Allies and they are enthusiastically greeted as a sign of friendship."

The Dutch Legation in London announce:
"Our appeal for aid sent to the Allied Governments has been answered. Britain and France are going to our assistance immediately."

Belgium, too, appealed for help. The Luxemburg Government have fled.

(Continued on PAGE TWO)

HITLER IS FOLLOWING THE SCHLIEFFEN PLAN—SPECIAL ARTICLE AND MAP, PAGE SEVEN.

You Must Carry Your Gas Mask
A.R.P. Should Be On Alert
—*Says Ministry*

The Minister of Home Security states that in the light of to-day's events in Holland and Belgium, it is very necessary that all civil defence and A.R.P. services should be on the alert.

The carrying of gas masks by the public is once more necessary. They should acquaint themselves with the position of shelters and first aid post in their neighbourhoods.

Householders are recommended to overhaul their domestic preparations against air attack.

Anti-aircraft guns over a wide area around the mouth of the Thames were in action at dawn to-day when five German airplanes, believed to be Heinkel bombers. flew over the coast and passed over several towns.

The sound of heavy firing awakened thousands of people, who hurriedly dressed and went into the streets to catch a glimpse of the raiders.

No air raid warning was sounded, but wardens were on duty and shepherded everyone indoors.

Five airplanes, flying in an arrowhead formation, were seen. They were flying at about 10,000 feet. Their course was clearly marked by the puffs and flashes of the bursting shells from the anti-aircraft batteries.

They were flying due east. A few

(Continued on Back Page, Col. Three)

The wish to remain neutral is shattered. © John Frost Newspapers/Alamy.

for the time involved, helped convince the government of the UK that the Netherlands would be a valuable future ally.

Although the occupying forces were supported by a minority of the Dutch population, the internal resistance movement soon came into existence and continued to grow during the course of the four years under occupation. Queen Wilhelmina and the Dutch Royal family left the capital of Holland, The Hague. They boarded the British destroyer HMS *Hereward*, from where they were evacuated to London where the Dutch queen took charge of the Dutch government in exile. Relationships with the Dutch government remaining in the Netherlands were tense, but she was extremely popular and sought to have the Dutch Prime Minister Dirk Jan de Geer, who intended to open negotiations with the Germans for a separate peace, removed. With the aid of a minister, Pieter Gerbrandy she was able to do this. Her late night broadcasts to the Dutch people on Radio Oranje were eagerly awaited, and she was described by Churchill as 'the only man among the governments in exile in London'. Many of the civilian population also attempted to flee the country, and the invasion led to a wave of suicides, particularly within the Jewish population.

As the German army continued its relentless march across Belgium and France to the English Channel, the Allied army that remained from the British Expeditionary force that had been landed in France following the invasion of Poland, was now forced to evacuate. They left for Britain from the beaches of Dunkirk from 27 May 1940. Although it was referred to as a 'miracle of deliverance' and gave rise to the famous Churchill speech on 4 June 'we shall fight them on the beaches', it was clear to the Dutch that the misery of occupation would last a long time.

The German high command had a problem in knowing how to deal with a country whose people were so similar racially and culturally to the Aryan ideal and in language. For example, the names Oma and Opa are exactly the same for grandparents in Dutch and German. The view of the SS Commander in Holland, Hans Rauter, an Austrian Nazi, was that Holland should be annexed and form part of Germany, to remove any last vestiges of Dutch identity. A curtain of suffering was drawn over the country for the next five years.

My mother was living at home and the family tried to carry on some semblance of normal life. We have no written accounts of this time from her apart from the letter she wrote for my niece Amy, but this gives a good indication of what the family were going through. My mother had always been a keen Girl Guide and when Amy was interested in the movement my mother wrote to her. In the first section of the letter is a description what was happening at the time of the invasion and how it stopped her guiding activities, before going on to talk about her time as a nurse:

At the end of August 1939 I was in a guide camp. We heard that England had declared war on Germany and we had orders to break camp and go home. I remember that night, everything was packed, tents included and we slept under the starry sky which was a new experience, but we were all a bit scared as we did not know what would happen. Holland kept neutral in the First World War, and we all hoped it would do so again this time. But the country prepared for a possible invasion, bridges were mined, trees pruned ready to fall and make barricades. Sure enough, on the 10th of May 1940 we were invaded. I lived near the German border and the village was simply overrun by a half dozen Germans on horseback, but soon followed by tanks. There was no fighting – no opposition. That started about 60 kilometres further on with the big river causing the hold up. But our small country was no match for the German army and after five days it was over, and we were occupied. In the small village where I lived there were no brownies or guides but I had started the grammar school in the nearby town, about six kilometres away and I had found the guides there. As soon as we were occupied scouting and guiding were forbidden as it was English based and we were given the choice to join the Hitler Youth. Nobody did. We carried on guiding secretly. We had found an old disused railway carriage in a field, and the kind farmer to whom it belonged let us use it. We were allowed to make a fire and cook meals there. Mashed potatoes through which we mixed cut up endives or carrots or onions. We could not wear uniform of course and never leave any evidence in the hut of what we were doing. Before long it became too dangerous and we had to stop our meetings. At school on the 22nd of February we wore a snow-drop and ivy-leaf so you could see who had been in the scouts or guides. But a year later into the occupation the Headmaster (understandably) had to put a stop to that!

World Thinking Day is celebrated every year on 22 February. It is a day when scouts and guides remember their brothers and sisters all over the world. It was chosen as it was the birthday of both Robert Baden-Powell, the founder, and Lady Olave, his wife.

I was told by my mother that after the German invasion, and the billet-ing, or occupation of the house by German officers, that Opa Holland, my grandfather, developed a rapport with one of the officers. Opa Holland was 'invited' to the part of the house that would have been his original sitting

①

At the end of August '39 I was in a Guide Camp. We heard the news that England had declared war on Germany, and we had orders # to break camp and go home. I remember the last night, everything was packed (tents included) and we slept under the starry sky, which was a new experience, but we were all a bit scared, as we did not know what would happen. Holland kept neutral in the 1st World War, and we hoped to do so again this time. But the country prepared for a possible invasion, bridges were mined, trees ready primed, ready to fall to make barricades.

Sure enough, 10th May, 1940 we were invaded. I lived near the German border, and the village was simply overrun by about a dozen Germans on horse back, but soon followed by tanks. There was no fighting — no opposition. That started about 60 km further on — with the big rivers causing the hold-up. But our small country was no match for the German army, and after 5 days it was over, and we were occupied. In the small village where I lived there were no Brownies or Guides, but I had started the Grammar school, in the nearby town, about 6 km away, and I had joined the Guides there. As soon as we were occupied scouting & guiding was forbidden (it was English based!) and we were given the choice to join the Hitler jugend. Nobody did!

We carried on guiding (secretly), we had found a disused old railway carriage in a field, and the

②

kind farmer to whom it belonged let us use it. We were also allowed to make a fire, and cooked a meals there. Mashed potatoe, through which we mixed cut-up endive (or carrots & onions) We could not wear uniform of course, and never leave any evidence in the hut of what we were doing. Before long however it got too dangerous, and we had to stop our meetings.

At school on 22nd Febr. we wore a snowdrop or Ivy leaf, so you could see who had been a Scout or Guide. But a year further in the occupation, the Headmaster (understandably) had to put a stop to that!

Mother describes her days as a guide.

room to talk in the evenings. Apparently Opa Holland grew to respect the officer, trying to see the situation the officer found himself in, not perhaps something all would sympathise with. It is difficult to comprehend this rapport given that Dick, my mother's older brother, was actively involved in the resistance movement, and was awarded a green beret, only worn by the Dutch commando forces.

We are not to know whether the discussions they had included the problem – or what was seen by the Nazis as a problem – of the Jewish population. If so, as we shall see, this would have been a difficult area for Opa Holland to discuss. Holland shared with the Scandinavian countries a modest degree of anti-semitism and although German Jewish refugees before 1939 had not received a particularly warm welcome, support and assistance for Jews was especially prevalent among the Dutch Calvinists. The negative feelings about the Jewish population were probably no more than those of other western European countries, with their roots in Christian teaching. Certainly by the spring of 1934, limitations were starting to be put on the numbers of migrants being allowed to settle, an uncomfortable comparison at the time I write this, as refugees flee Syria and the near east. However, the dreaded and feared persecution of the Jewish population that was expected by many soon gathered momentum in the early war years, and in February 1941, after widespread arrests of Jews, in Amsterdam the Communist Party of the Netherlands called for a strike in protest against this new law. It lasted two days and was the first public demonstration against Nazi Jewish policies in wartime Europe. Many citizens of Amsterdam joined in this mass protest against the deportation of Dutch Jewish citizens and factories in other cities were shut down. However, the occupying Nazi regime was able to crush most of the local Dutch resistance, firing on unarmed crowds and taking many prisoners. The strike was over within two days. They were aided in the programme of deportation of the Jewish population by the National Socialist Movement, a group that was initially not notably anti-Semitic, but under the leadership of Anton Mussert became active in helping find Jews in hiding. Sections of the Dutch police force also at times played a vital and deliberate part in the removal of the Jews. This was particularly the case in Amsterdam, home to the majority of the Holland's 140,000 Jewish population, where the charismatic wartime superintendent Sybren Tulp was a fervent admirer of Hitler. The Dutch members of those organisations may not have been initially aware of the final destination of the victims, but it must have soon become clear of what was happening. The 'razias' or round-ups of the Jews increased in intensity and in 1942 transportation to the concentration camps began. The Dutch Jews were moved on trains to Westerbork, in

The fenced-in Jewish quarters in Amsterdam.

the north east of Holland, and the first train left Westerbork for Auschwitz on the night of 14 July 1942. The deportations in Holland turned out to be a catastrophe unparalleled in any other western European country, with between 70 and 80 per cent of Dutch Jews ending up in the death camps in Poland.

The Rutgers family was one of many in Holland who sheltered Jewish refugees fleeing persecution and possible deportation, or the many children of parents who had gone into hiding or already been deported.

The story of 'cousin Fransje' goes as follows:

At the beginning of the war, Dr Jacob van der Hoeden was teaching bacteriology in the academic department of the hospital in Utrecht. After the Germans occupied Holland, one of his students, Henry (Harry) Cooymans, left his lecturer a note which read:

'Knowing that you are Jewish, and that you may get in trouble, I leave you my name and address. You can contact me whenever you may need help.'

When the deportations of the Jews in the Netherlands began in summer 1943, Dr van der Hoeden was faced with a difficult decision. Believing that the best chance for survival was splitting up the family, he had to separate

This photograph of three girls taken in Vriezenveen, on the lawn of the family home, shows my mother kneeling behind her sister Rikje and 'cousin Fransje'. In fact cousin Fransje De Jager was really Rahel van der Hoeden, pronounced Rachel in Dutch, the daughter of Jaap, a friend and colleague of my mother's father Evert Rutgers.

from his children. Being in different hiding places meant that the parents didn't know if their children were safe. Children were taken from their families and brought to strangers where they would remain for long periods of time, totally isolated from parents and siblings.

The two young daughters of the van der Hoeden family, Rahel (Fransje) and Jaqueline (Lieneke), age 13 and 9 respectively, were taken in by a family, but soon their hiding place became unsafe. Their father remembered his former medical student and contacted Harry and Alice Cooymans, who immediately offered to help and shelter the girls in their home at Sint-Oedenrode, in the province of North Brabant. Rahel and Lieneke stayed with the Cooymans family from October 1942 until April 1943. The two girls were presented as members of the family, and treated as such in all respects. They studied, helped decorate the Christmas tree, sang Christmas carols, occasionally went on walks in the woods with the three Cooymans children (aged seven, five and three) and their nanny, and attended daily evening prayers. Their true identity was kept from their school friends and neighbours. Only Harry and Alice knew the girls were Jewish.

In April 1943, a Dutch police officer warned Harry and Alice that the Germans had become suspicious of the girls and were planning to investigate their identity. Many years later Alice told her foster daughters that the most difficult thing she had to do in her entire life was to tell van der Hoeden that his daughters had to move into another hiding place. The two sisters had to separate. Rahel was taken by Jacob to Dr Sieb Numans, a veterinarian in Ede, in the province of Gelderland, who had just married Gerrie Rutgers, my mother's older sister, a former scientific analyst in Jacob's laboratory in Utrecht. Gerrie and Sieb sheltered the young girl under the guise of 'cousin Fransje' in Ede for approximately six months before things became too dangerous. She was then put on the train to Vriezenveen, to join the Rutgers family where she stayed during the summer, before moving to another address for the rest of the war.

She would certainly otherwise have been one of the many hundreds who wore a yellow star and whom my mother described in her newspaper articles as seen cowering at Utrecht station before transportation to Auschwitz or Belsen. At the time of the photograph, my mother must have been on a visit to the family home, aged about 20, while sister Rikje was still living at home. It astonishes me even now that her arriving and staying for so long was neither questioned nor discovered.

Rahel survived and the van der Hoedens went to Israel in 1948. Rahel was visited by my cousin Mattijs, the son of Sieb and Gerrie Numans, in the summer of 2010. Mattijs took his family with him and Rahel was able to tell them of her escape, by taking the train from Utrecht to Ede and then on to Vriezenveen.

LEFT: One of Israel's highest honours, the Yad Vashem, was awarded posthumously in 1995 to my uncle and aunt, Sieb and Gerrie Numans, on behalf of the Rutgers family, several of whom were able to attend the award ceremony in The Hague in 1995.
RIGHT: The cover of Tami Shem-Tov's moving account of Lieneke's story.

My mother had been invited to the ceremony, but was unable to travel then. One reason the story can be so well remembered is that a book has been published, *Letters from Nowhere*, written by the Israeli author Tami Shem-Tov, based on the real story of Lieneke, Rahel's younger sister. This fascinating and emotional story describes how she was delivered letters written by her father while secretly hiding in Nazi occupied Holland. The letters were filled with love and laughter, illustrated and bound together in booklets.

> The village doctor gave Lieneke the first letter after teaching her how to make cough syrup and Lieneke never imagined that there was a letter from her father in the pocket of Dr Kohly's black jacket.

His illustrations show the care and love Dr van der Hoeden was able to express and each letter was accompanied by the words 'destroy after reading', which fortunately did not happen and a good number of letters were preserved.

If all this is true heroism, there is another side to the story of the Jewish children who were sheltered, away from their families in the years of the war, and the consequences that followed. It is the subject of the effects on the children in having to come to terms with their survival in these circumstances.

The story of Anne Frank is of course known worldwide, following the publication of the diary written between 1942 and 1944 of her experience of being in hiding at 263 Prinsengracht, in Amsterdam. While not the capital, Amsterdam was certainly the most important city in Holland and conditions were particularly brutal especially during the Dutch Hunger Winter of 1944–45. The Frank family went into hiding in July 1942, just under a month after Anne's 13th birthday, when she had been given the present of a square notebook that became her diary. The first entry is two days later and it is worth noting that if she had had close friends to confide in, the diary would never have been filled with her thoughts. The difference in the story I am recounting, of the actions of the Rutgers family in sheltering the young refugees, is that they were not hidden, but both ways held equally dire consequences if the truth were revealed. Sadly, in the case of the Frank family, that did happen as they were betrayed in August 1944, to be transported via Westerbork to the concentration camp at Bergen-Belsen where Anne died in March 1945.

Beyond Anne Frank: Hidden Children and Postwar Families in Holland was written after the author Diane Wolf became aware of the difficulties experienced by some of the children at the end of the war. Some six decades after the end of the war, she undertook close to 70 interviews with those who had been 'hidden children'. Her focus was on family dynamics, particularly the experience of surviving in relative comfort, while members of their family might have met a terrible fate. The main theme was a feeling of guilt and identity problems, and of course the readjustment to being reunited with any members of the surviving natural family after hostilities ceased. They were survivors of the Holocaust in a different way. It is a complex study, and in part erodes the myth of the perceived Dutch altruism and the established narratives of this chapter in Dutch history.

Another intriguing chapter in my mother's time during the war years took place just before she was about to leave the family home to commence her nurse training. Yet again the family took frightening risks to help children under threat of deportation. My sisters had told me, before I learned more from my cousin in Holland, that my mother had also worked at what she described as a 'special school'. She stayed with the family of Betty Cadbury-Boeke in Utrecht, probably for some months before she commenced her nursing training. The Cadbury-Boeke family were also many years later to be honoured by the government of Israel, and their names inscribed on the Wall of the Righteous, the monument built on the outskirts of Jerusalem.

Fiona Joseph's book tells us:

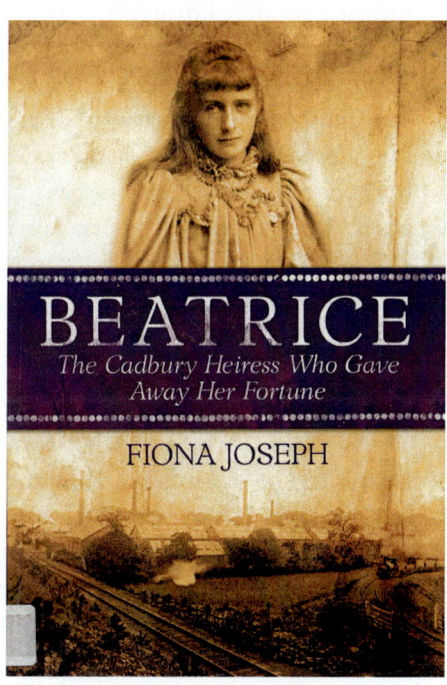

Born in 1884, Beatrice (Betty) Cadbury belonged to the world-famous chocolate empire founded by Richard and George Cadbury. They formed the company to be known as Cadbury Brothers and as business stabilised they positioned cocoa as a health drink with great success. When new premises were needed, the Bournville factory was built. From a very early stage in development provision for the welfare of the workers was made, large dining rooms to serve nutritious foods and dressing rooms for the workers to change clothes. Richard was able to move his family to

The story of Beatrice Cadbury has now been told in a book *Beatrice – The Cadbury Heiress Who Gave Away Her Fortune*, written by Fiona Joseph, a story of the astonishing journey from respectable Quaker girl to marriage and peace activism with her Dutch husband 'Kees' Boeke.

Moseley Hall where the birth of Beatrice took place. She grew up in a fine mansion with servants, a good education and the chance to travel and see the world. As Richard became wealthier he had the challenge of reconciling this with his Quaker beliefs and he took civic charity duties seriously as well as a commitment to the Gospel Temperance Mission. The Cadbury girls were brought up to be aware of a world outside their own privileged background. Quakerism remained central to her father's life, alcohol and gambling of course forbidden but tragedy ensued in 1899 when Richard died in Jerusalem having contracted diphtheria. He was surrounded by his family, who had travelled with him on this expedition to the Middle East. The company was dissolved, a new limited company formed and shares issued to all family members. Those of Beatrice, a mix of Ordinary and Preference shares, were put in trust for her until the age of 21. In 1903 Beatrice moved to London to study at Westfield College, a women only academic institution, but after completion of her studies it was her turn to be the dutiful daughter and she returned home to be with her mother. However in 1920 she gave back all her inherited shares to the Bournville factory workers. This was a dramatic step and the family were thrown into conflict, but she was not to be dissuaded. From being a respected Quaker girl she became a peace activist, having met and married Cornelius 'Kees' Boeke, a Dutchman. Cornelius Boeke had found inspiration from Bournville, the garden village the Cadbury family had built for their workers, having met his future wife during his training in Birmingham as a missionary. The couple had relocated to Holland at the start of the First World War, after travelling and working as missionaries. By the early 1920s the couple had begun to withdraw from the peace movement and formulated their ideas of a school 'de Werkplaats' (the workshop). The school was to be at Bilthoven near Utrecht in Holland. It opened in 1929 and was to follow an ideology of the pupils as 'workers' whose own needs and motivation would form the basis of their education and learning process, with the teachers as 'helpers'. Beatrice and Kees eschewed the use of money. The 'Break with the State Doctrine' was a rigid and uncompromising position but as they became aware of the difficulties this caused for both their children and the school, reluctantly agreed to allow the Boeke Trust Committee to help fund the school. They believed the answer to a society they hoped to create lay in education. Kees thought there should be no rewards or incentives, that children would not be given marks or grades to record their achievements and that children at the school should be multi-lingual.

An issue that caused tension for Beatrice and Kees at the school was the demand of the German occupiers in September 1942 that all schools give the names of all non-Aryan children to the authorities. Jewish children were already being transported to the holding camp at Westerbork. Beatrice felt that to comply with this would have been entirely against the spirit of unity in the school, the school would close down and all the children would suffer.

Others including Kees disagreed, judging that the school should remain open and that the act of giving a list of names was comparatively harmless – some of the children already had false identity papers. It was decided then to give the names of the Jewish children to avoid closure of the school. Beatrice had her own concerns as she lived in dread it might be discovered she was English, but there was another reason. She had taken into her household two Jewish children. The children had fled from Breda in the south of Holland and took the assumed names of Jan and Liesje. They were integrated into the school life of the Werkplaats but always had to be on their guard. In 1944 the school was requisitioned by the Germans, and it became too dangerous for the children so they had to move on. The family endured the harsh winter of 1944–45 and the clandestine activities continued until Kees together with Stella, the school secretary, were taken into custody. It transpired that a young lodger in Stella's house was Jewish and a member of the resistance. In prison the young Jewish man told his captors that they – Kees and Stella – were unaware of his identity and role. The young man was shot while Kees and Stella were thankfully released.

My mother wrote of her time there just once, briefly to my sister Jane and her daughter Amy.

Dear Jane and family, I have just spoken to you and am sending the article straightaway so that Amy can have a look at it as well. When you come over in October you will have to see the scroll, it is very impressive. I thought the article was good, because I told him so much, he said enough to write a book, but then you never know what's going to appear in print. The paragraph where he says 'the children would arrive in the dead of night' that was when I was at that special school near Utrecht with Betty Cadbury, where we had regular night visitors. Poor kids frightened eyes in little white faces, plenty of bed-wetting, there are some things you never forget. The same as that scene on Utrecht station. I don't know if you saw the TV programme on Hitler last Sat. Second part this Saturday. I was not going to watch it but it was very compelling how he portrayed Hitler

Jews pitilessly deported to Westerbork.

going quite mad and hysterical and how he swept up a whole nation in his hatred of the Jews. Carlisle (of *Full Monty* fame) was the actor.

The school clearly had a very different function during the wartime years, and as my mother says in her account 'some things you never forget'.

A few months after the spring of 1945 when the war had ended, Betty and Kees could return to the Werkplaats to restart their work. The decision taken by Princess Juliana, returned from her exile in Canada, to send her three young girls to the school for their primary education was a crucial point in the reestablishment of the school and its educational principles.

Many years later Mattijs, my cousin in Holland, attended the school, now of course much changed and conforming to mainstream educational values. Mattijs still lives in De Bilt near the village of Bilthoven where the original school was built – another family connection with the school.

The card shown on p. 36 was sent to my mother following a concert held in the Werkplaats school, to raise funds for the school. The concert was performed by the children of Leominster Junior school, the school where my father was the Headteacher, with much of the organisation of the trip being undertaken by my mother. Over 70 children travelled to Holland to perform at the school. We are now sure that my mother worked in the Werkplaats school in 1943, before she left to commence nurse training. Betty Cadbury

THE VISIT TO HOLLAND

The School Party leaves England on May 27th for the week's stay in Holland.

Preparations for this visit have been going on for a year. In the past, parties from School have made regular Journies, to such places as Ireland and Scotland, and have taken part in Cruises. The plan for a Journey to Holland was well received, as was the idea of "taking our music" with us.

Gradually, by contact with schools and churches in Holland, and by personal contact which Mrs. Cartwright, Dutch-born wife of the Headmaster was able to effect, a programme has been built up and arrangements made.

We are grateful, and also proud, that this Journey has been approved, and supported financially, by Herefordshire Education Committee.

The parents of children involved have given steady support throughout, and by your presence here tonight you are helping in some degree.

A primary purpose of this Journey is that the children should make real contact with Dutch people and children. At our first afternoon Concert in Woerden, schoolchildren will form the audience. An unusual experience will be that of entertaining on the Promenade at Scheveuingen—a well-known resort near The Hague.

The visit to the Kees Boeke School, De Bilt, near Utrecht, is of particular interest. The school was founded by Kees Boeke, husband of Betty Cadbury, with whose family Leominster has strong connections. Mrs. Cartwright worked at this school for some time during the War. It is now a large Comprehensive type school of some 800 pupils. Here we are to give a short afternoon Concert to younger children, be entertained to tea, and join with Dutch children in an evening Concert.

On our last day the Brass Band will play at Evensong in the English and American Episcopal Church, The Hague. Again refreshments are kindly provided, and we shall give a few secular items in the Church Hall before leaving for the boat.

The party will stay at a Civic Youth Centre, "Overvoorde", in The Hague. Visits are arranged and the canal trip in Amsterdam is a natural choice, as is an evening visit to the model village of Madurodam. A full day's journey takes in a cheese market and a typical Dutch fishing village.

In all these activities, as the Education Committee has made clear, the School is acting as an ambassador for Herefordshire. Moreover we are carrying the name of Leominster abroad. We hope that many Dutch people will come to know and respect the name because of the activities of this School during this coming Whitsuntide.

The visit made by Leominster School to Holland.

clearly remembered her well, as the postcard shows how pleased she was to see her again, and meet her English husband.

While all this was happening in my mother's life, sheltering the young girl 'Fransje' and the time spent at the Werkplaats school with the Cadburys, the

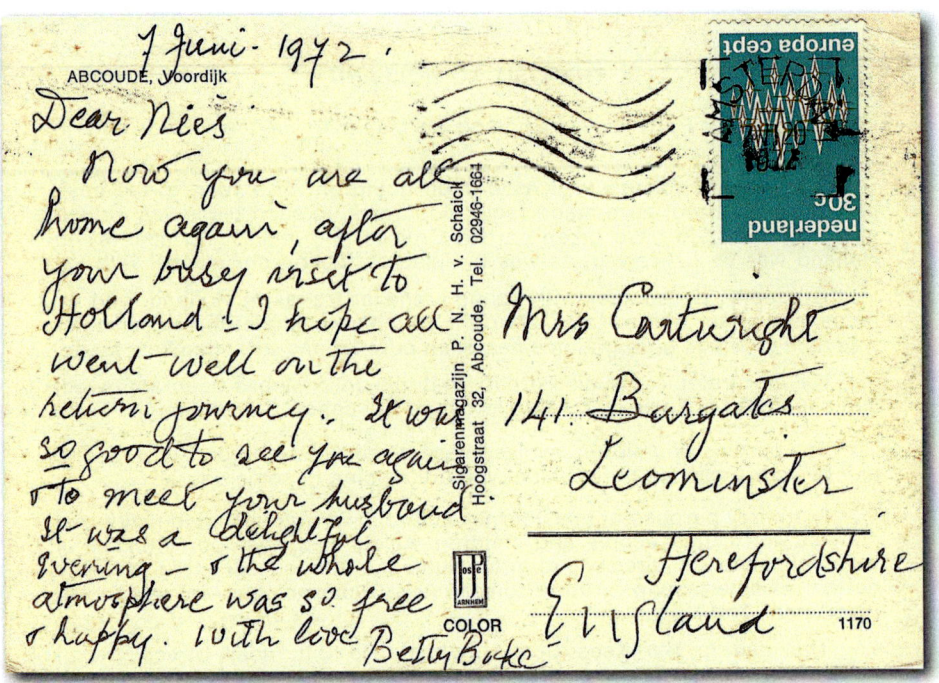

After my mother died my sister recalled there was a postcard sent to my mother by Betty Cadbury in 1972, some three years before Betty died and we were able to locate it in my mother's effects.

national disaster being inflicted on Holland continued. In those early years of lost freedom, the country was ransacked, factories dismantled and shipped to Germany, radio, press and political parties were given over to the collaborationists and 400,000 people were shipped to Germany and compelled to work for the German war effort.

In May 1943 there was a general strike in Holland when the Germans sent back to POW camps Dutch soldiers captured in the spring of 1940 (but who were due for repatriation to Holland three years later). One hundred and fifty Dutch civilians were killed in savage reprisals by the occupying forces. It is against this background that my mother was to commence her nurse training in Velp and the experiences she had undergone helped us understand her opening comments in her account of her time there, in the first of the newspaper articles she wrote.

However, by this point, the time my father was to spend in Iceland was coming to an end. He had seen no fighting action by the end of 1942 but that was to change. He and the 4th Lincolns were posted back to the UK to begin further military training.

CHAPTER FIVE

The 4th Lincolns and my father return to England, 1942

We returned to England in December 1942 and took a night train from Glasgow to Hereford and I went to 'A' company training young recruits. This went well for some months until I was returned to the ranks, for the heinous crime of returning late back from leave! At this I applied to join the mortar platoon where Lofty and other friends were settled. Much training followed in Scotland and Suffolk.

My father wrote up the date of return of the 4th Lincolns to the UK as December, but the date was actually in September, noted from several sources.

I had often wondered what the different labels or markings on his old kitbag and rucksack were for. They were stored in the attic of our house, with an old silk parachute which, I recall, we later made into a kite – with the light material it worked very well. The kitbag was inscribed with the letters 'Sergeant' and the huge rucksack was imprinted Corporal, which was of course the rank he had in the Training Corps. I began to wonder if there

The mortar platoon. My father is middle row, second from the left, his beret at a jaunty angle.

It must have been at this time, before he joined the mortar platoon, that my father attended a PE course in Aldershot. In the photograph, he is back row, second from the left.

really was a 'heinous crime'. Mystery solved, back late from leave! The paragraph explains why he was a Private in Iceland (as we note from the caption in the list of players in the Northern Lights Orchestra concert), then a Corporal after returning to the UK responsible for the training of young recruits, with another change of rank to follow later in the story.

The 4th Lincolns Territorial Army Battalion formed part of the 146 Brigade based at Hereford and Ross-on-Wye. There was intensive training and the mortar platoon had trebled in size to 40 men, with three sections each having two 3 inch mortars. My father spoke about his time in Herefordshire with more fond recollections than the rest of his time in the war. He was attracted to the countryside, talked of his visit to the town of Ludlow and of course some 30 years later was to return to the county to take up his final teaching post.

In the spring of 1943 the 4th Lincolns moved to Scotland to begin training in combined operations and assault methods. The battalion moved from Comrie, in Perthshire to Rothesay, on the Isle of Bute. They practised assaults on beaches from landing craft and storming blockhouses while under fire from live ammunition.

This could only mean one thing: preparation for the invasion of Europe had started.

In July 1943 command of the 49th Division was handed to Major General E. H. Barker nicknamed 'Bubbles' Barker (the nickname referred to his effervescent spirit). He instilled a new aggressive spirit through the division and one of his first acts was to change the emblem. He decided the Polar Bear should now have a raised head, irrespective of the fact that a Polar Bear in preparing for attack lowers its head.

The two insignia showing (above) the original and (below) Major General Barker's new version.

In December 1943 the 4th Lincolns were moved with the rest of 49th Division to East Anglia and were billeted at a holiday camp in Kessingland, Suffolk. It was a grim and bleak time, with no heating or lighting in miserable accommodation. In December 1943 General Dwight D. Eisenhower was appointed Supreme Allied Commander for the invasion of Europe. General Sir Bernard Montgomery was to return to England to command the 21st Army group, the force designated as the initial invasion force, the date of which and of course the landing area in France being unknown to the troops. Intensive training continued and involved all vehicles being waterproofed and continually tested. The 4th were instructed in flame throwing, clearing mines and street fighting. 'Monty', as he was known, made a point of visiting all his troops, followed by the King who reviewed them at Somerleyton Park. Visiting this beautiful area (although Kessingland still struggles in this respect) with the wide skies, peaceful Norfolk Broads and the splendid Somerleyton Hall it is difficult to visualise this happening all those years ago.

During this time my mother had been accepted for her nurse training in Arnhem, and her life changed dramatically.

CHAPTER SIX

The Hospital at Velp, 1943

A nursing career starts

The stories that tell us most about my mother's experiences during the wartime years were based on the time she spent in Velp, in the hospital where she commenced her nursing training in the autumn of 1943. I recall visiting Arnhem in 1957, with my parents, a very different city from the ruined one of 1945, and have a memory of two of her fellow nurses Toot and Ote being there for an emotional meeting. My mother described in her letter to Amy (see Chapter 4), which began with the story of her Girl Guide activities, how she started work and training in the hospital:

When I had done my equivalent of A levels it was difficult to decide what to do. The universities had all been closed, that is to say, you could study but had to sign a declaration that you would be loyal to the occupying forces. And very few students did that. I had always been interested in medicine so I went in for nursing, initially in a children's hospital in Arnhem. When I was old enough (18) I went to a suburb of Arnhem to start my training. It was a small hospital (about 80 beds). You knew everybody, which was a good thing in view of the difficulties to come, after the Battle of Arnhem in September 1944. In the hospital we kept contact with the ex-guides and scouts (some of the younger doctors) and organised walks whenever possible.

My mother enrols as a nurse in Velp.

I mentioned in my introduction the series of newspaper articles. These were published in the *News Chronicle and Daily Dispatch*, a national daily paper, in September 1956. Earlier that year, my mother had answered a request for readers to send in letters relating to their wartime experiences. If selected they would be published. I was old enough to remember the story and her disappointment about her own not being chosen. However, she was contacted by the paper and a journalist called Mary Hampson visited our house in Whitwell. They became friends and the articles were drafted and published as a series entitled 'Woman of Arnhem', spread as a series over just one week. They tell her tale much better than I am able to, and were of course the original inspiration for this story:

News Chronicle and Daily Dispatch Monday September 17th 1956 Woman of Arnhem Part One, by Nies Cartwright-Rutgers.

I'D forgotten what peace was like until I went to Velp Hospital, about four miles from Arnhem. But there, in the autumn of 1943, I walked right out of the war—or so I thought.

I remember the first time I saw the hospital on the day matron accepted me as a student nurse.

It was a lovely day. The sun was shining, and the other nurses made me feel immediately at home—or maybe it was the hospital.

From the moment I saw it I loved it. It was as if peace and security and happiness had been mixed with the mortar and the bricks. It was more than a house, it was a home, and the whole staff made the family.

That first day, the nurses who were off duty went mush-rooming, and I went with them. When we got back, we fried them and took some for matron, and that surprised me. I never expected a woman who could be so dignified and approachable; so efficient and yet so willing to share in any fun.

Her initial interview had been a searching inquiry into my education, family and background, but none of the questions she asked was political. She was looking for a good nurse, and that's what I was hoping to be.

I was thrilled that she had accepted me. Velp had a fine reputation as a teaching hospital.

There was accommodation for about 100 patients, including a number of private cases, and a staff of 70 or 80, and that first day, and for many days after, I thought I was just another nurse in just another hospital.

We worked hard, because matron would settle for nothing less than efficiency, but she had a way of making the simplest, most menial task seem significant and important, and the most inexperienced nurse feel necessary. She was always busy, and she always had time . . .

I realise now that when the youngest nurse on night duty took matron her early morning tea—as she always did—and perched on the edge of the bed to give a report on the

WOMAN OF ARNHEM
Part One
by NIES CARTWRIGHT-RUTGERS

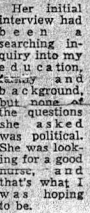

NIES CARTWRIGHT-RUTGERS would not like to be called brave.

NOW she is an English housewife, married to a schoolmaster with Robin (10), Jimmy (6) and the twins Barry and Anna-Marie (3) to complete her happiness

THEN she was a nurse in Arnhem, fighting death and the Germans together. Her father and brother were members of the Resistance. Her home had been commandeered by the Germans . . . Here she tells a new and wonderful story of Arnhem.

night's happenings, she told matron far more than she thought.

Matron learned as much about the nurse as the nursing, and that was important. It was a matter of life and death that she should know and trust her staff. We were fighting far more than disease in Velp. We were fighting the Germans as well.

I'm not sure when I began to realise that Velp was no ordinary hospital. I think it was when I was washing the medical orderlies' white overalls.

The boys in white

Joop de la Tour and William were not the only boys in white; there were overalls for Tjomme, the local butcher, Jan the baker, and Henk, who was an insurance agent before the Germans came.

I thought it a little odd, but I was glad of their help and I never asked questions. That was one of the first lessons I learned in Velp.

Then I noticed that the boys used to disappear at night in an ambulance which Wolter, another of the orderlies, had fitted with a home-made generator.

They came back with food and supplies and sometimes stranger cargoes. Sometimes they came back with a patient for the private patients' ward.

Slowly it began to dawn on me that Joop's dark eyes saw far more than the Germans ever knew.

I began to learn a little about some of the private patients, too.

Communist forger

Mr. Bernard, for instance. He was a dramatic-looking man, with a mop of grey hair and burning brown eyes, and his chart didn't make his condition clear. After all, there is no medical name for the sufferings of a Communist under a Nazi regime, and Mr. Bernard had nothing wrong with him that victory wouldn't cure.

His chart said that he was sick, but he was always well enough to forge official papers, provide reliable addresses for escaping prisoners, wrap up food parcels to be smuggled into the prison in the town,

I'd forgotten what peace was like until I went to Velp Hospital, about four miles from Arnhem. There, in the Autumn of 1943, I walked right out of the war – or so I thought. I remember the first time I saw the hospital on the day the Matron accepted me as a student nurse, and from the moment I saw it I loved it. It was as though peace and security and happiness had been mixed with the mortar and bricks. It was more than a

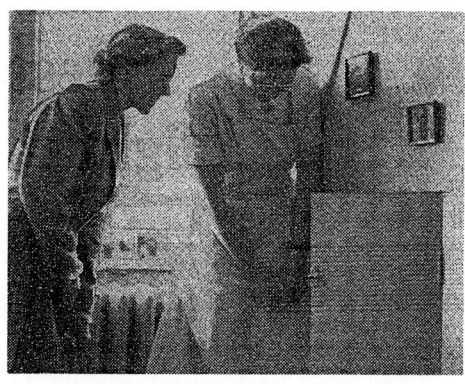

My mother revisits Fenna's room, with the false panel, an escape route for 'the boys'.

hospital: it was family and home. That first day we went mushrooming, and took some back for Matron which surprised me, I never thought such a dignified and efficient woman could have such a sense of fun. Her initial interview had been searching, questions about my family and background as well as education, but nothing political, she was just looking for a good

Fenna, Henk and children.

nurse and I was thrilled to be accepted in a hospital with such a good reputation. Matron knew as much about the nurses as the nursing, which was important if she was to trust her staff. We were fighting much more than disease in Velp, we were fighting the Germans as well. I think I began to realise the hospital was no ordinary hospital when I was washing the medical orderlies' white overalls. Joop de La Tour and Willem were not the only boys in white. There were also overalls for Tjomme the local butcher and Henk who was an insurance agent before the Germans came. I never asked questions – that was one of the first things I learnt. The boys used to disappear at night in an ambulance driven by Wolter, another orderly. They came back with food and supplies and strange cargoes, sometimes a patient for the private patients' ward, about whom I began to learn a little. Mr Bernard was a dramatic looking man. A mop of grey hair and burning brown eyes. His chart did not make his condition clear. There is no medical name for 'Communist suffering under the Nazi Regime'. There was nothing wrong with him that victory would not cure. His chart said he was sick, but he was well enough to forge official papers. These provided

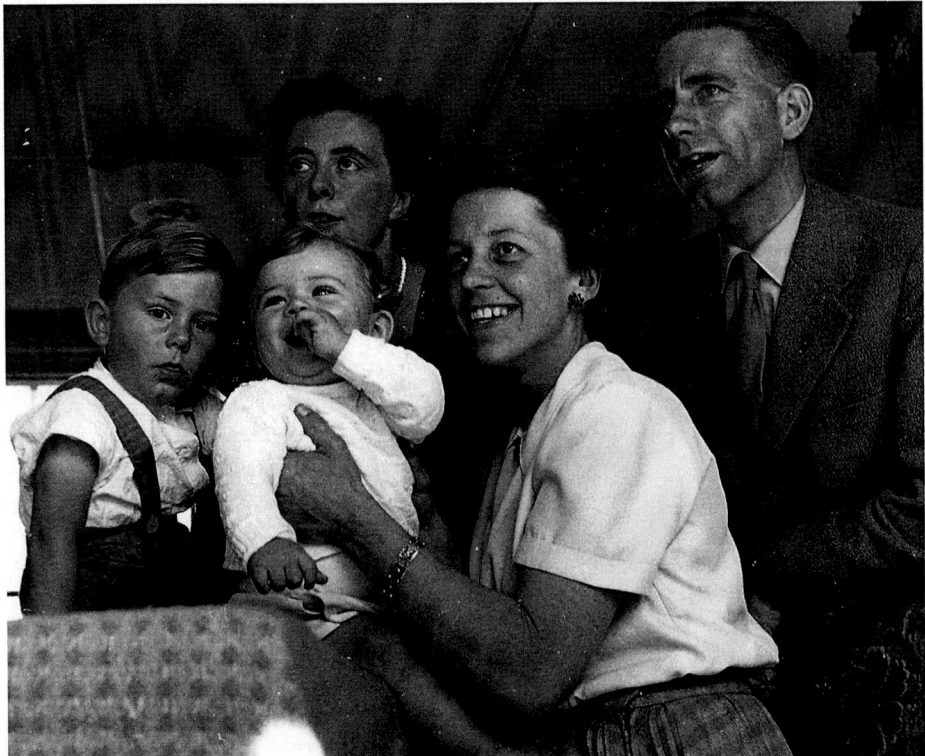

Meeting Wolter and Dinni and family.

Meeting the Onderduikers again: Tjomme and his wife.

reliable addresses for escaping prisoners. He helped arrange crazy concerts for us, which we held in the cellars. The Germans would have been very interested in these: we made costumes from gauze and bandages, and Mr Gerritson supplied the tunes. He was a violinist performing on Dutch radio before the war, German by birth but Dutch by inclination, but had not been naturalised in time. His stomach trouble remained interminably acute, and he was 'confined' to his room for long periods. Calmly I was drawn into the other side of the hospital – the cloak and dagger war. By the time I discovered the false panel in Nurse Fenna's room, through which the boys were occasionally compelled to disappear at the double, it was no longer a shock to me.

This then was the first instalment of the series that was written for the paper in 1956, and it will help to explain some of the story that my mother recounted.

The 'Onderduikers in Het Wit' was the name the hospital gave to Joop, Willem and the young men in white, who took part in the resistance

Dutch men walking in a line – 'slave labour on the way to Germany'.

activities. Literally the name means 'Underdivers in White'. The underdivers were those who went into hiding to avoid capture, or enforced transport to Germany to work in factories or elsewhere to aid the German effort.

With my mother's effects that we found after her death, was a card, or invitation, that had been made for a meal and small concert on 4 May, when fighting would have just ceased, immediately before the signing of the unconditional surrender. The menu was written in hand and I think was a recognition of the Onderduikers and their heroism during their time in the hospital.

The dangerous clandestine activities continued through the spring and summer of 1944 until the false dawn of September 1944 and the failed attempt by the allied forces to liberate Arnhem in Operation Market Garden. My mother describes that time, with the hopes that were raised and the dis-astrous outcome of that battle, in her second newspaper article. During this first year of her time in the hospital, my father and the 4th Lincolns were preparing to take part in the D-Day invasion of France and see their first action of the war in the horrendous fighting that was to ensue in Normandy.

CHAPTER SEVEN

Normandy, June 1944

The Allied invasion, D-Day and beyond

On 28 May 1944 the 4th Lincolns had been put on six hours' notice to move, and on a Sunday morning, 4 June, they moved with the battalion by train to a marshalling area near Lewes in Sussex.

The 49th Division, the Polar Bears, became the follow up to the 50th Division, which had made the assault on Gold Beach on D-Day. The Lincolns embarked from Newhaven just before midnight on Friday 9 June and reached the French coast at midday the following day. Their military hardware of trucks with Bren Gun carriers had been loaded up in the London Docks, to be transported separately. My father wrote:

> We embarked for France from London in 1944 and landed in Normandy on D+4, it was originally D+1. All was quiet – except for those on the carrier which began to sink and they had to swim for it.

As my father says, the expectation was for the 49th Division to land on D+1 but, possibly because the advance into France had not reached its targets, or because of delays offloading the troops and equipment already on the beaches, the landing was delayed. The Lincolns must have been stunned by the scale of what they saw, and shocked by the scenes of destruction on the beaches as they set foot on land about midday on 10 June.

There are innumerable books, films and accounts of the dramatic events of 6 June, and the days after. It is impossible in this story to convey the magnitude of the event. My father had never spoken about it and would never watch television or films that showed the scenes of the battle so I cannot elaborate. Suffice to say that those who came ashore safely went inland as soon as possible. The 4th Lincolns cycled to Coulombs some seven miles inland, leaving their cycles there, never to be used again, and the battalion were held there until 12 June when the anti-tank guns and vehicles arrived

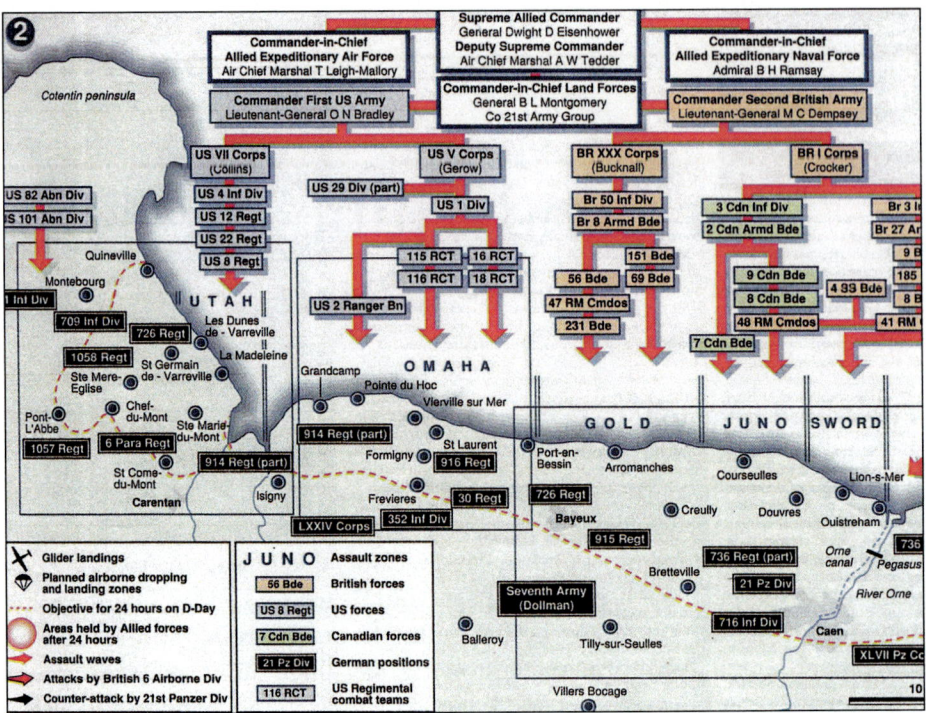

D-Day 6 June – the invasion plan.

at Coulombs. From there the plan was for the 4th Lincolns to move further south, to the front line.

A day later, on 13 June, the 4th Lincolns were now up to strength after the chaos of the landing and they reached an area about a mile and a half north of a small town called Tilly-sur-Seulles. They were now in 'bocage' country – thick hedges with roots so big the tanks could not move them, and steep banks alongside narrow winding lanes.

My father describes in his account the preparations the mortar platoon went through as they prepared for action:

> The routine for some 2–3 months was to dig your own slit 'trench' (6' x 3' x 1'6"), but after you had dug the large circular pit for the mortar. The mortar was used to fire a shell a foot long and four inches wide. It was transported along with shells and 5 men on a bren gun carrier. There were three parts to it, all heavy, the base plate, the frame and the 3' barrel. The frame had a mechanism by which the barrel could be raised or lowered and swung right or left.

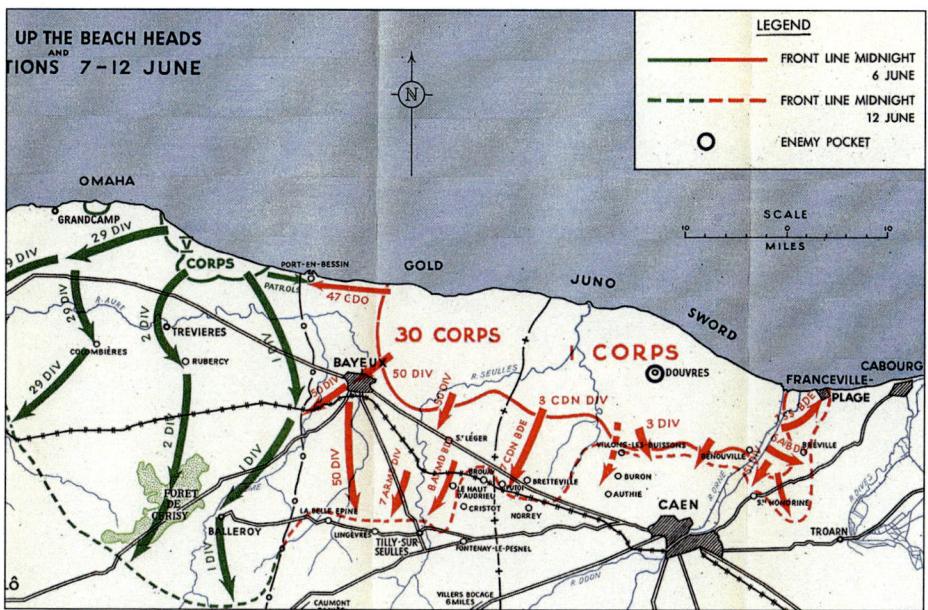

Allied positions, 7–12 June.

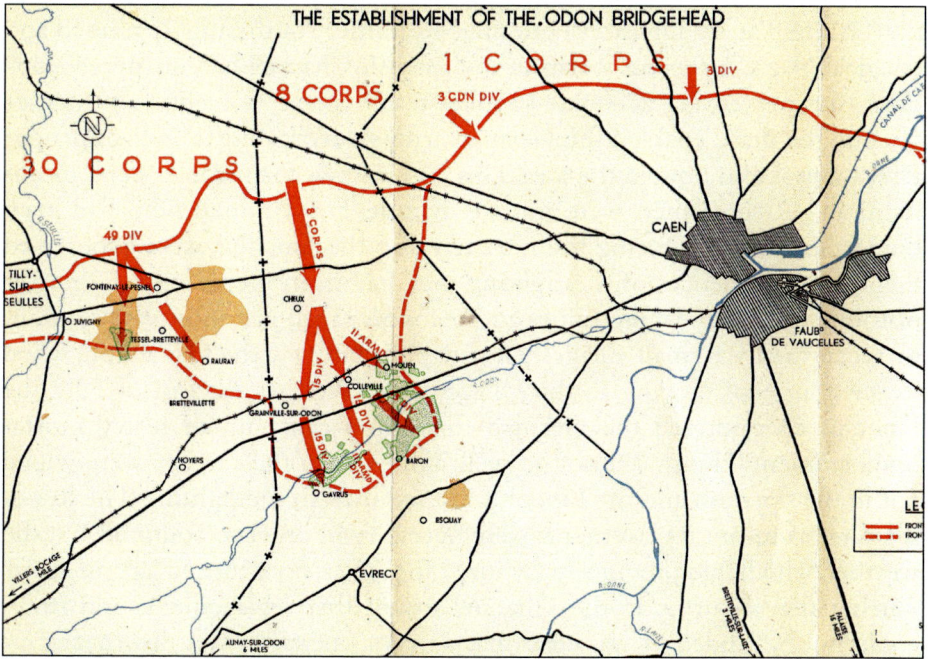

The route to Tilly-sur-Seulles for the 49th Division.

British infantry unit firing through a gap in the 'bocage', © Pictorial Press Ltd/Alamy.

The men were soon to see their first action. The troops facing them were the 12th SS Panzer Division Hitlerjugend (Hitler Youth), highly trained and fanatical Nazis. A furious storm in the English Channel had disrupted shipping, thus preventing adequate supplies reaching the front line and consequently the delay enabled the German army to reorganise. The Panzer Lehr Division was also now in the area. This division was formidable. 'Lehr' means training, but these men were not the recruits but the men who had been doing the training. During the next ten days the Lincolns were exposed to their first experiences of the fighting they had been preparing for. Pioneer platoons were busy laying mines and reconnaissance platoons were sent out to 'recce' the local small villages. Thursday 15 June saw the first action, when in the course of moving to the village of St Pierre, north east of Tilly, the Lincolns encountered the German forces and came under heavy mortar bombardment. Things did not go well; almost all of the carriers were wiped out in the skirmish and the Lincolns lost ten men in the fighting. The loss of the carriers meant replacements were necessary in order to continue, but the weather, which had previously favoured the Allies, now turned against them. Further fierce storms in the Channel meant that replacements and stores could not be landed. It was clear that a major operation was now necessary to take forward the advance.

Montgomery had decided to launch an attack, code named Operation Epsom, with the main attack taking place between Tilly and Caen on 26 June. The 49th was to attack early on Sunday 25 June, to allow V11 Corps to pass through and try to reach Caen from the south west. The 4th Lincolns were on the extreme right of the three infantry battalions mounting the attack. They would be attacking Bas de Fontenay on the western outskirts of Fontenay village. It was vitally important for them to capture the Juvigny and Fontenay area on the western outskirts of the village.

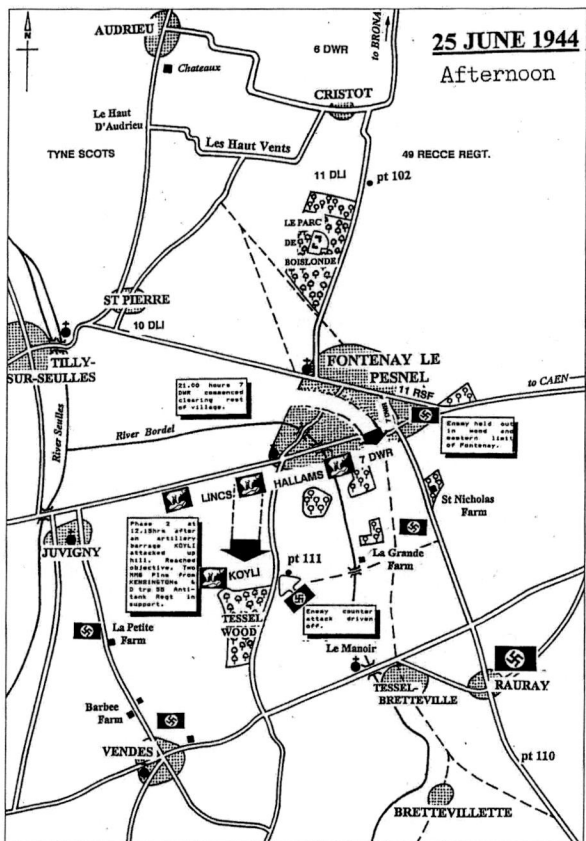

ABOVE: The area of the Fontenay battle.
RIGHT: *The Times's* report of the Tilly battle.

BRITISH ATTACK IN CALVADOS

ADVANCE BEYOND TILLY

FOREST WARFARE

From Our Special Correspondent
CHERBOURG FRONT, JUNE 25

Before first light of this glorious Sunday morning British formations on the Calvados front began an advance against limited objectives east of Tilly-sur-Seulles. Since the definite capture of Tilly a few days ago there has been little movement in this sector apart from constant patrol clashes in the woods and sunken lanes.

Even for the smallest attack the pattern is the same. At 3 a.m. a heavy artillery

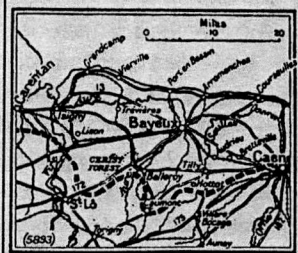

barrage of guns—field, mediums, and heavies—was put down on the enemy astride the River Seulles, in an area 1,000 yards deep. It is a French military maxim that forest warfare is a voracious *mangeur d'hommes*, and indeed this savage bombardment must have brought the trees down about the enemy's ears. It lasted for 45 minutes, and then our infantry began to creep forward through a thick ground mist.

With dawn came the fighter-bombers to add their weight of destruction on German positions. The whole plan was concerted with such care and power that Panzer units that have been in the line ever since the landings and have been mercilessly whittled down could do little to prevent us from advancing.

The fighting continues, and for an hour or more from its opening, allied heavy bombers in large formations droned over the enemy's forward positions to attack the vital communications behind them.

1,000 YARD ADVANCE

WITH THE BRITISH FORCES, June 25,—British infantry, after less than four hours' fighting through close wooded country, this morning advanced over 1,000 yards south-east of Tilly. The advance, in which no armour was committed by either side, began shortly before 4 a.m. The battle is said to be going on "very satisfactorily," and though German tanks are known to be in the vicinity they have not yet shown up. The drive has taken British troops to an important point south of Tilly.—*Reuter.*

The Battle of Tessel Wood and Fontenay

It is difficult now to imagine, in the peaceful Normandy countryside, the horrendous scenes at the time. One event my father relayed to me was, for a long time, all I knew about his experience, and was pivotal to his time in the forces. The action on 25 June 1944 was the first live fighting action he and his mortar platoon had been in and sadly, for many in that platoon, the last. At dawn the action commenced. In poor visibility the Lincolns started to creep forward, with deafening noise surrounding them, the early morning mist becoming heavily laden with smoke as platoons began to lose touch with each other. It was all very frightening, and there was hand-to-hand fighting with the enemy. Finally, the Lincolns were able to get on with the urgent job of digging in. The fighting was extremely fierce. My father did talk about it just once. During this period of heavy artillery barrage the mortar pit in which the platoon had tried to shelter took a direct hit from shellfire. He told me how he tied an ID tag to the body parts of Sergeant Danny Huddlestone, his closest friend in the forces then, who was killed instantly in the attack:

> Our first action, and one of the worst, began about 4.00 a.m. on June 25th, the attack on Fontenay. We reached our position, a large barn and orchard, dug the mortar pit, when we were hit by shells, whining in and exploding. This, and being our first time, was very frightening, and went on for 20 minutes A strange quiet then, and we expected a follow-up attack. Nothing. As we emerged and took stock, it was bad. On that day 14 of the battalion were killed, and 7 were from the mortar platoon. Enough of that.

The whining shells my father referred to were from the 'Nebelwerfers', the German six-barrelled mortars firing 15 cm rockets. They were known as the 'Moaning Minnies' or 'Screaming Minnies' because of their dreadful noise and were the weapon the troops came to fear the most.

A paragraph from the book *Saturday Night Soldiers*, page 104, describes the events of that day:

> In an orchard the mortar platoon were getting into position. The circular pits were dug and the mortars placed. Suddenly all hell broke loose. Shells and mortar bombs fell all around them, and the men dived for cover. It was the most intensive barrage of mortar and artillery fire the men would experience in the whole campaign. A bomb landed in the pit which Fred Illing was in and Driver Tomblin took the full force of the bomb and was killed, but Fred and the rest of the men were unhurt. Captain Waters and

Sergeant Huddlestone were on the outside of the pit shouting some-thing when another mortar bomb burst where they were standing and they were blown to bits. Rubble and stones trickled into the mortar pit, followed by Captain Waters' glasses, still intact. Seven men in the mortar platoon had been killed and a further five wounded, so the loss to the platoon was devastating.

A look at the Roll of Honour of the 4th Battalion, the Lincolnshire Regiment, confirms that 14 men were lost, including Sergeant Daniel Huddlestone. This figure is the highest the regiment had for any one day in the whole campaign. Much has been written about the Normandy campaign – the bitter fighting, the name Polar Bears being given to the division and the conflicting stories told regarding decisions not to take prisoners. The account above brings home the very personal emotional trauma he and his comrades went through.

'Enough of that', were the words my father used. That same sentiment, the reluctance to talk of those men who fought in the forces during the war and who survived to talk about their experiences, is a theme I have come across so much in reading and examining the stories and accounts of these horrific events. My father would not have wanted to talk about the stories that have been recorded, the suggested failure of the allied troops to obey the rules of the Geneva Convention, the decisions to shoot prisoners rather than take them alive. However, he remained a very tolerant man, for when I returned home after my first year at university, wearing a beige ex-army overcoat, pur-chased from the Laurence Corner store in Hampstead Road, London, sadly no longer there, he refrained from comment, although it must have been an unwelcome reminder of the past.

Writing poetry has been a means of expression for those men both in and about to take part in battle, knowing that they themselves or some comrades could die. Constructing a poem, drawn from the thoughts going through the minds of the soldier during moments of peace and calm must have given some comfort.

The Second World War produced more poets than the Great War of 1914–18 and their words are often as powerful, although they do not represent the dire and sanguine consequences of a static war of attrition. They have yet to become more widely known. I am sure one day they will.

One poem that is very moving to read was written by John Jarmain, a captain in the 51st Highland Division. He was killed in Normandy at Sainte-Honorine-la-Chardonne on 26 June, one day after the death of Sergeant Danny Huddlestone, from my father's platoon. Although written by Jarmain in the desert sands at El Alamein, it has words that would resonate with my father as he visited the grave of his friend 50 years later.

At a War Grave
No grave is rich, the dust that herein lies
Beneath this white cross mixing with the sand
Was vital once with skill of eye and hand
And speed of brain. These will not re-arise
These riches, nor will they be replaced;
They are lost and nothing now, and here is left
Only a worthless corpse of sense bereft,
Symbol of death, and sacrifice and waste.

On the 50th Anniversary of the D-Day landings, in 1994, my parents travelled to France and visited for the first and only time the area where this battle had taken place and my father paid his respects to his fallen comrades in the cemetery at Tilly-Sur-Seulles. I recall my mother telling me that the organised bus route had to take a detour to this particular cemetery and how my father was given time to alight from the bus and search out and visit the grave of his fallen comrade, Sergeant Danny Huddlestone, alone and in quiet reflection.

So to return to the Normandy Campaign and Operation Epsom. The 4th Lincolns continued to hold their position and finally succeeded in their objective. There was praise from Major General 'Bubbles' Barker, who recorded the words 'The Battle of Fontenay was the 4th Lincolns' Battle'. As well as the 14 killed in battle, some of the 64 men who had been wounded died later, while others suffering badly with battle exhaustion, barely able to speak, had to be taken away from the lines. However, the fighting had to continue, as my father recounts:

There followed a period of digging in, firing, sleeping in slit trenches until we took up a position near Caen, in reserve. From there we were moving forward fairly easily and I saw the first civilians. As we moved up a long sloping field there was a house which had to be investigated. It was utterly shattered. Near the fireplace sat an old lady. She was quite still, just sat and stared. There was nothing we could do, the follow up troops would take care of that, but it all seemed so hopeless. As it did at Breuil-en-Auge when we took the carrier out to bring back some wounded from the fighting there and found a young boy of about 11 who was completely lost – we brought him back to the first aid post.

November

1st	Private C Bourne	Died
17th	Sergeant E Dunk	Died

1944
June

15th	Private R Andrews	Killed in action
	Corporal G R Baxter	Killed in action
	L/Corporal J Elliot	Killed in action
	Private T S Oakes	Presumed killed in action
	Sergeant F L Peacock	Killed in action
	Private A W Preston	Killed in action
	Private D Thorold	Killed in action
	Private J Waddle	Presumed killed in action
	Private F Wright	Killed in action
	Private J York	Died of wounds
16th	Lieutenant J D Gaunt	Killed in action
17th	Private J T Baker	Died of wounds
18th	Private A G Wink	Killed in action
21st	Private J Halton	Killed in action
	Private R Howells	Killed in action
23rd	Private P Major	Killed in action
25th	Private J A Brewster	Killed in action
	Private C C Carpenter	Killed in action
	Private J Crosby	Killed in action
	Private E A Davies	Killed in action
	Private C Golland	Killed in action
	Private D Hoyle	Died of wounds
	Sergeant D G L Huddlestone	Killed in action
	Private J Hughes	Killed in action
	Private B Lambert	Killed in action
	Private H Petch	Killed in action
	Private W A Settle	Killed in action
	Captain L F Sparks	Killed in action
	Private H C Tomblin	Died of wounds
	Captain D W Waters	Killed in action
26th	Private C Ashton	Died of wounds
	Private R Bailey	Died of wounds
27th	Private J R Bealey	Died of wounds
	Sergeant E Fell	Killed in action
	Private J Haywood	Killed in action
	Private R Hodson	Killed in action
	Private S J Taylor	Died of wounds
29th	Private L Allen	Killed in action
	Private H R Hudson	Died of wounds
30th	Private J Jones	Killed in action
	Major J M Staniland	Killed in action

The Lincolns killed in action, 25 June.

The German losses were heavy and they were stunned. Lord Haw-Haw on German Radio had coined the phrase 'Polar Bear Butchers', again a reference to the perceived policy of the allies to take no prisoners and which subsequently inspired the design of the 49th Division Christmas card. I found one in my father's effects; it was blank and never sent. Knowing him as we did, he would never have used or sent such an image.

From the book *Saturday Night Soldiers* we know:

> The 4th Lincolns were now holding a position near Fontenay, and as the battalions were rotated they were allowed a respite period from the front line. They were withdrawn to the village of Ducy-Sainte-Marguerite, not far from Coulombs, where they cycled to after landing in France. Some of the battalion were able to go to Bayeaux. Records show they next went to Démouville, now a suburb of Caen. They must have traversed the area south of Caen as it was not yet liberated.
>
> It was a wretched place, totally ruined. There had been many French casualties. From there it appears they were redirected south to the commune of Airan, to hold a position north of the cauldron of the 'Falaise Pocket'.

The Battle of the Falaise Pocket, fought from 12 to 21 August 1944, was the decisive engagement of the Battle of Normandy. It took its name from the area around the town of Falaise. It is also known as the Battle of the Falaise Gap, this being the corridor that the Germans sought to maintain to allow their escape. The German Army Group B were encircled, trapped and destroyed in this strategically vital area, leaving another scene of mass carnage. The victory here destroyed the bulk of the German forces west of the River Seine and left the way open for the advance east to Paris. However, fortunately the 4th Lincolns were not directed south to fight there, and were spared the horrendous sights of destruction in the Falaise area. Instead, the next move was back north again. The 4th Lincolns advanced along the eastern side of the ruined city of Caen to Sannerville, just north of Troarn. It is little wonder my father commented, in the opening paragraph of his account of his wartime experiences:

> At times in Normandy it was difficult to remember where you were, or even why, so these are just memories.

The area around Troarn had been the scene of some earlier fierce fighting. The reason was that the area was bounded on its east by the River Dives, with its numerous bridges. It was important to destroy these to protect the eastern flank of the Allied bridgehead from the German forces. The most important of these was at Troarn. The action and events are described in *Red Berets into Normandy: 6th Airborne Division's Assault into Normandy D Day 1944*, a book written by Huw, later Sir Huw, Wheldon, the well-known BBC TV broadcaster.

On 26 August the Lincolns were on the move again, now heading north from Troarn. They crossed the River Risle and reached the Seine at Quillebeuf-sur-Seine, about 20 miles west of Rouen, and then moved west to Le Havre. My father recorded:

> As we moved forward to Le Havre I remember the swarms of mosquitoes near Troarn and a broken down house with a BED still intact and the feeling of lying down on such a thing. The attack on Le Havre went comparatively easily though our infantry had to use flame throwers. By now we realised our mortars were always positioned behind the front line, an obvious benefit, but equally they were an obvious target for shelling.

My father's written account doesn't really fit the events recorded in books written about the wartime battles of the Polar Bears. Le Havre was heavily defended by coastal artillery batteries with a large garrison of German troops. The Lincolns were the advance guard of the division and the action consisted of several battles over a period of 12 days. The Lincolns made their HQ in Harfleur, and suffered 14 casualties.

The Germans surrendered Le Havre on 12 September, and the Lincolns left the following day, leaving behind a shocked distressed populace, but one still able to publish the newspaper *Havre Matin*.

Following the liberation of Le Havre, orders were to proceed to Lille, in the far north-eastern corner of France. Then on 17 September the disastrous Operation Market Garden commenced. Market Garden was the code name given to the action taken by the Allied forces in their first attempt to liberate the still occupied north-eastern area of Holland. The epicentre of the action was the city of Arnhem. There was dispute between Montgomery and the Supreme Commander, General Eisenhower, regarding the overall strategy. The latter wanted to advance on a broad front. Montgomery was disappointed not to command all the Allied forces to the final victory. However, he managed to get Eisenhower to agree to Operation Market Garden – the brilliant and daring idea to seize bridges over the rivers Maas, Waal and Neder Rijn using the combined forces, to clear the way for the armoured columns to drive 60 miles north, deep into occupied territory. The thinking behind this strategy was that it would cut Holland in half and isolate the

Part of *Havre Matin's* front page for Wednesday 13 September 1944.

Germans in the west of Holland, establishing the British army across the Rhine, within striking distance of the Ruhr. It was a gamble, one that was to fail in its objective and a time of heartbreak for the Dutch population still under the misery of occupation.

That heartbreak was shared by my mother and all those in the hospital as hopes were raised by the sight of the parachutes and the sounds of battle and fighting in the streets of Arnhem – tears of joy to be followed by tears of sorrow.

The operation was planned at Moor Park, a Palladian mansion near Rickmansworth, Hertfordshire, now the home of Moor Park Golf Club. The first floor room in which the details were planned is now named the Arnhem Room, decorated with framed photographs and a large flag depicting the wings of the Red Berets.

CHAPTER EIGHT

Arnhem, 17 September 1944

The first Battle of Arnhem and hopes of liberation

'The Red Devils are here, the Battle Begins' is the title of the second article from the newspaper series.

The parachutes weaved down on to the land on September 17th, the first day of the battle for Arnhem. The throb of the engines made a solid wall of sound beneath the sky. I stood on the roof of the hospital and we cheered for those men who could not hear us, and wept for their courage. Briefly we forgot the longer war we were fighting with our treatments and temperature charts as we heard the barking of guns in the streets of Arnhem a mile or two away. We rang St. Elizabeth's, the large hospital in Arnhem and

WOMAN OF ARNHEM – 2

The Battle begins

By NIES CARTWRIGHT-RUTGERS

With her wartime companions Wolter and Dinie, Nies Cartwright-Rutgers (centre) looks out over the Peaceful Rhine and remembers that 12 years ago, this was the battlefield.
Picture by *News Chronicle Dispatch chief photographer William Bradley*

'Operation Market Garden' and hopes are dashed.

a voice that was strangled with excitement said 'they are in St. Elizabeth's fighting, it can't be long'. They were the British, and it was freedom. Those five days of battle were a confused memory for me, as rumours swept through the hospital. The patients could not move, and when we said 'cushions ready', they had to put the cushion over their head and slither down into the bed. But this is also the story of the hospital, the boys in white – and some of the men they saved. Men such as Harold Riley from the sedate holiday resort of Lytham St Anne's, one of the paratroopers who jumped out at 500 feet over the city to swoop into houses firing sten guns and rifles, and wondering, when they had time to think, when the big guns they had been promised for support would come.

The attempt to cross the Rhine in September 1944 – Operation Market Garden – has been well recorded and filmed as *A Bridge too Far*. The film illustrates the mistakes made by the Allied Command, notably underestimating the German force (thought to comprise mainly old men or Hitler Jugend) and the problems that the 'follow on forces', the infantry, would face in trying to reach the city of Arnhem through the narrow and only road into the city. After several days of house-to-house fighting, the paratroopers were killed, captured or driven back, alone in the battle with no support arriving.

Some like Harold Riley, mentioned in my mother's account above, were sheltered by resistance workers. He was one of the lucky ones. His story is recounted in my mother's final article when some weeks after the failed operation he met Jan, one of the 'boys' and Margot, a nurse from the hospital, who assisted him in hiding and helped provide the papers and forged passports on the route to freedom.

One not so lucky was Harold Bennett, the father of one of my old primary school friends.

I mentioned Ralph, his son, earlier in this account and the coincidence by which we started to communicate, not having seen each other for over 50 years. His father Harold was a paratrooper, who took part in the first attempt to secure the bridge across the Rhine, in September 1944, and was severely wounded in the attack. His experiences describe what the paratroopers had to do and what the outcome was for so many who took part in the landings. It also shows the debt of gratitude felt by those in the forces who were protected and cared for by the Dutch nurses and resistance workers.

This is Ralph's account as he sent it to me:

Dad flew out by glider transport on the second day and he tossed a coin with his comrade to decide who would descend into battle, but lost. After

The Red Devils parachute in to Oosterbeek.

crashing they found the foe was waiting for them, and had cut off the bridge. Father and his mates, the Military Police, diverted to the Hotel Hartenstein in Oosterbeek where he stayed for the rest of his part of the campaign. Almost 3 days later he was severely wounded (right arm/elbow and femur) and taken into cellars by the Dutch women who cared for him and nursed him as best they could. Eventually he was evacuated to the Sint Elisabeth Ziekenhuis in Arnhem, where he was almost sentenced to summary justice by the SS as he was wearing Dutch togs after his paratrooper smockdress had been removed in order to operate on him in the cellars. (Anaesthetic was the contents of a bottle of Oude Genever – Dutch gin – administered by a glass and funnel.) He regained 'compos mentis', showed his dog tags and red beret and that saved his life. Eventually he was evacuated to Appeldoorn and eventually to Lingen across the German border. It was there he experienced a generous expression of humanitarian aid on the morning of 6th December, when the German Red Cross nurses/protestant nuns came into the civil prison ward and placed a lighted candle at the foot of each bed – it was S. Nicholas Day. Eventually he was moved to Fallingbostel and the terrors of Stalag 11b, where he was to stay until liberated on 14th February 1945. On Easter morning (before Liberation) a fellow POW (Captain Dick Bonham-Carter – a famous family) presented each patient in the 'hospital barrack' an egg – INCREDIBLE. During this time my mother was declared a widow many times after Dad had almost been given up missing, presumed dead. The Reverend Sternberg (Rector of St Lawrence Church) called to soothe her every day. She received a telegram towards the end of April 1945. That summer she received a small piece of brown paper via Geneva, signed by Dad and handed to a Dutch nurse or resistance worker in the military hospital in Apeldoorn. My father always had the greatest of respect for the Dutch and especially for your mother who translated Dad's military documents for the Whitwell GP Dr Sam Evans, who shared his surgery with Dr Gerald Wood in a small building in Fox Road just behind the Methodist Church where we had our school class in 1956–7 with Miss Dennet, and later Graham Taft. In 1994 I went as a guest for the 50th Anniversary of the Battle for the City. That's part of Mum and Dad's story in a nutshell. I visited Arnhem as a guest for the 50th Anniversary of the battle for the bridge – a bridge which Dad never saw.

Many years later, I was to come across Richard Bonham-Carter, to whom Ralph refers in the account. He had been a medical officer attached to the 4th Paras, and was also to end his war years as a POW. In the mid 1960s, I was a medical student in London and part of our paediatric attachment was a teaching visit to the world famous Great Ormond Street Hospital. At that point Richard Bonham-Carter was a nationally famous cardiac physician,

With Toot opposite St Elizabeth's in 1956.

who pioneered the work on 'blue babies' and the intensive care they need. I have a distinct recollection of our group being shown the wards by him, a totally different experience from the usual formal visit. He almost ambled through the wards, waving though glass doors to patients, completely at ease with everyone. His obituary records that he also spoke little of his time in the war, or the POW experience, other than to say that it was the parachute jumping training that led to the lifelong back problems that he experienced

At the Hartenstein Hotel in 1956.

The losses suffered in this first Battle of Arnhem were horrendous. 156 Parachute Battalion was based in the lovely area of Melton Mowbray, in the Leicestershire countryside. Of 603 men who flew out from Saltby airfield to take part in the battle, only 37 returned. Their story is told in the book *From Delhi to Arnhem: 156 Parachute Battalion*. The author was John O'Reilly, whose father, also named John, survived the ferocious eight-day battle and was part of a group of soldiers who existed for three weeks behind enemy lines after the initial attack.

The ground forces of the Allied Army were never able to cross the Rhine in sufficient numbers to relieve the paratroopers who were overrun by 21 September and the river remained a barrier until the offensives of March 1945. The hope that the war would end by Christmas was gone; many of the British forces had more fighting to do before reaching Arnhem.

Bridges were blown up by the retreating German forces.

In his book *Normandy to the Baltic*, Field Marshall Montgomery claims this first operation to liberate Arnhem was 90 per cent successful, based on the crossing of the Waal and Meuse and establishment of a ground force on the 'Island', the small waterlogged piece of land where my father spent the freezing cold winter of 1945. The operation could be considered of course a total failure, as the objective was to get across the Rhine. Better to have agreed 'a bridge too far' before rather than after the operation. In the book of that name by Cornelius Ryan, the penultimate page is headed 'A Note on the Casualties' and makes stark reading:

> 'Allied Forces suffered more casualties in Market Garden than in the mammoth invasion of Normandy. Most historians agree that in the 24-hour period of June 6th, 1944, total Allied losses reached an estimated 10,000 to 12,000. In the 9 days of Market Garden, combined losses, airborne and ground forces, in killed, wounded and missing, amounted to more than 17,000. British casualties were the highest, a horrendous total of 13,226.
>
> What were the Dutch civilian casualties? No one can tell. Deaths in Arnhem and Oosterbeek are said to have been low, fewer than 500, but no one knows with any certainty. Conflicting stories give contrary information and suggest the civilian casualty figures (dead, wounded or missing), may have been as high as 10,000, a result of both the Operation Market Garden campaign and the subsequent forcible evacuation of the Arnhem sector leading to the starvation in the terrible winter following the attack.'

I have no military background or training, but this does not sound like a 90 per cent successful mission. Certainly the failure to cross the Rhine prolonged the war into and during the bitter winter of 1945.

My mother continued her account in the newspaper series, the second of the articles concluding as follows:

> On the second day of fighting the refugees arrived and we were crowded with new casualties. One of the saddest sights I shall see was old people and young children pushing all they had in baby carriages and hand carts. In the hospital we could only wait, the pattern of the 3rd and 4th days was unchanged. The rumours continued, but by the 5th day we knew they had lost.

However, the work of the hospital needed to carry on, the Dutch 'Honger Winter', the hungry winter of 1944–45, was about to begin, and the allied infantry, including the 49th Division, which included the 4th Lincolns, continued to make progress across Belgium towards Holland.

CHAPTER NINE

Antwerp-Turnhout, September 1944

The 4th Lincolns from France to Belgium and over the Antwerp-Turnhout canal

While the hopes raised by the attempt to take Arnhem were crumbling away, the Lincolns left Le Havre and continued north east across France. They moved a few miles east of Le Havre to the village of St-Aubin-Routot for a rest period until they left on 19 September, heading initially north towards Dieppe on the coast, but before arriving there they were redirected again to reach Lille on 21 September. The following day they travelled 90 miles to reach Kessel just south of Antwerp, and finally on 24

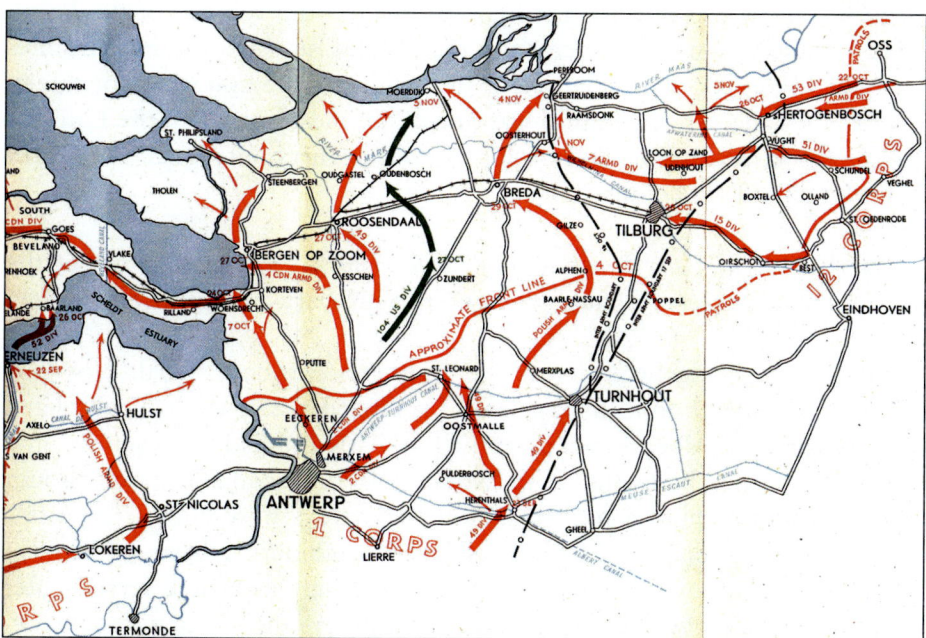

The Antwerp-Turnhout canal.

September moved on to Oostmalle, just south of the border with Holland. They had orders to prepare to cross the Antwerp-Turnhout canal. My father writes in his account:

> The crossing of the Antwerp-Turnhout canal involved much more trouble, and the mortars were very busy. For the first and only time one shell misfired, and plopped gently out of the barrel into the mortar pit. Three men moved very quickly. It would have been useless of course had it exploded. At Poppel the Germans counterattacked and I remember running for the mortar pit, bullets whining thorough the air. Luckily the Germans were repulsed and I remember a two-day rest in the grounds of a monastery, and an eerie quietness.

John Benson in *Saturday Night Soldiers* does give a more detailed account:

> Although not wide at this point, establishing a bridgehead on the other side of the river was not easy, and the flat surrounding area provided little cover. The crossing was made at night, the Lincolns fearfully and quietly paddling across the canal. By daybreak they had infiltrated the German lines. There was sporadic fighting, and behind the defensive positions occupied by the Lincolns the Engineers were able to get their Bailey Bridge up, with vehicles crossing by first light. By 6 a.m. the vehicles of the Polish Armoured Division were crossing the canal. Elsewhere the Hallamshires and the Royal Scots Fusiliers came under intense fire, and were not able to cross the canal. The operation was one of the most important the Lincolns undertook, and the battle honour 'Antwerp-Turnhout Canal' was added to the regiment's colours.

In the book *The Polar Bears: Monty's Left Flank* are recorded some of the entries made by General 'Bubbles' Barker in his diary and on 27 September:

> We have a bridgehead across the Antwerp-Turnhout canal. Not bad. Since Div. March from Dieppe area, on Thursday 21st we had completed 2 bridges over Albert canal by early a.m. 24th and had a bridge over the Turnhout canal by 6 a.m., 25th. We took 10 offrs. and 508 men prisoner and wounded quite a packet. I must say we are now complete professionals. Everything works like well oiled machinery. I have a Canadian Armoured regt. with me and the CO made the unsolicited remark after being 24 hours with us, that he had never enjoyed working with any formation so much.

The following days were spent moving forwards and by 2 October the Lincolns reached Ravels, some three miles north of Turnhout, staying overnight at the Chapel St Jean. It is this location my father describes as the monastery grounds in his account. The 'rest' was necessary as the Hallamshires had reached the village of Poppel, before the Lincolns continued their progress to take part in the Battle at Poppel Forest on 6 October.

I have always felt that my father recorded in his account the least about the most difficult battles – an inverse law almost. He mentions only that the Germans attacked and were repulsed, whereas in his diary of 8 October General Barker records:

> One of my battalions (the Lincolns) had the devil of a battle with very obstinate Boche from midday on the 6th to late yesterday morning. Some 600 or so tried to infiltrate around them through the woods by day and night and they fought them off. We stonked the Boche with everything we had and two counter attacks were put in to relieve troops who had been surrounded. They must have killed 200 or more. Our casualties were very light in comparison.

Likewise, *Saturday Night Soldiers* reads:

> The Lincolns advanced from Poppel to Goirle the next day, supported by a lively squadron of Canadian Shermans whose simple but effective method of protecting the infantry was to shoot at everything. Progress was slow. The Lincolns came under heavy shelling and mortar fire and enemy resistance stiffened. By nightfall they were almost surrounded by the enemy, some only two or three hundred yards away. Orders came to withdraw, which they thankfully did. There was at least a brigade of Germans attacking the battalion, pounding the Lincolns.

The battle lasted throughout the night of the 6th and the morning of the 7th of October – clearly a major engagement for the Lincolns and so much more than my father recounted.

Records show they had been in action continually for two weeks, with 22 of their number killed and 74 wounded. Although the 49th Division had not moved far since crossing the Antwerp-Turnhout canal, a firm bridgehead had been established.

The 4th Lincolns were on the southern border of Holland and waiting to see where they would next be directed. I can only speculate how much the infantry knew about the failed Operation Market Garden attack on Arnhem in Holland. The allied forces had advanced further than expected in September – and although Montgomery and Eisenhower disagreed about strategy, 'Ike' was persuaded to support the daring plan. While the Lincolns had fought through Belgium in September, my mother and her nursing colleagues tried to come to terms with the misery of the failure of the first attempt to liberate Arnhem.

CHAPTER TEN

Arnhem, 23 September 1944

23rd Aftermath and the magic of one red beret

As the people of Velp recovered from the nearby battle, my mother and friends ventured out through the deserted streets of Arnhem. She wrote in her third newspaper article:

> We went down into Oosterbeek when the battle was over. It was a crazy dangerous thing to do of course as it was out of bounds. But it was a crazy world we lived in… We walked through the woods and looked out over the deserted town – red, yellow and green parachutes hung over the buildings like bunting over a carnival town; white crosses marked where the brave men lay. I was with Truus, another nurse, and we were trying to find some traces of her parents who lived in Oosterbeek. We found the house. It was split from top to bottom, the way you can split a log with an axe, hundreds of books had been blown down the staircase, and in the garden we found the Blue Delft China, in the cabinet, in the orchard, three inches deep in mud. One cup was still intact and suddenly the pain was almost unbearable. For me that little cup held all the futility and waste and misery of the war. We couldn't find the parents of my friend Truus, and no one could give us any news. We walked through the woods back to the hospital. It seemed the war would never end.
>
> In the hospital there was no room for misery or time for despair. We had more patients than ever, and more staff. Five doctors from Elizabeth's in Arnhem had joined us, we were all as dangerously involved as we could be. Conditions were worse – we had no electricity or light apart from the carbide lamps the boys had made us, little fuel and no hot water. The bombing was incessant, and the boys continued to disappear at night, each time they went out there was a chance they would not return. Yet they decided we should have a dinner party. One of the Arnhem doctors had salvaged some good wine. It was decided that there should be a meal to

WOMAN of ARNHEM—3
THE MAGIC OF ONE RED BERET

NIES CARTRIGHT-RUTGERS
continues her story of Arnhem. It is the story if the Red Devils' heroism and of the courage of the Dutch men and women who daily risked death to help them.

WE went down into Oosterbeek when the battle was over. It was a crazy, dangerous thing to do because it was out of bounds. But it was a crazy world we lived in, and we'd never acquired the habit of observing enemy rules.

We walked through the woods because it was safer that way, and looked down on the deserted town. Red, yellow and green parachutes hung over the battered buildings like the bunting over a carnival town.

Maroon berets were in the dust, so were the crosses which marked where brave men lay.

Torment

It was quiet and still and lost, and then we heard the clump of soldiers' boots as a German patrol came near, and we hid.

I was with Truus, another of the nurses at Velp, and she was trying to find some traces of her mother and father who lived in Oosterbeek.

We found the house. It was split from top to bottom the way you can split a log with an axe. Hundreds of books had been blown down the staircase, and one of them was open at a painting by El Greco. I can see it still, the lovely livid colours and the torment.

In their garden we found the Blue Delph china. I don't know how the cabinet had got into the orchard, but it was

Nies Cartwright-Rutgers, now an English housewife, returns to her native Holland to pay homage to the men who died at Arnhem 12 years ago.

cuse for one of the crazy, incongruous things which were always happening at Velp.

We were all as dangerously involved as we could be; conditions couldn't have been worse in the hospital—no electricity, no light, apart from the carbide lamps the boys had made, very little fuel and no hot water.

The bombing was incessant, and the boys worked in the wards each day and disappeared at night, and each time they went out they took a chance on their return.

Yet they decided we must have a dinner party.

Beautiful

One of the Arnhem doctors mentioned that he had managed to salvage some very fine wine. "Wonderful," said Joop. "That's just what we need, but we must have a meal to give it proper respect."

The doctor and his wife had

map on the wall which showed the German fortifications on the Rhine.

When he got back to the hospital he drew it neatly for future reference.

At night the boys would disappear. A band of men had come from Arnhem with the doctors. They slept in the children's ward in the day time, and we never asked what they did, nor where they went at night. Then one of them brought us a red beret and a tin hat for a souvenir—the owner had been smuggled to safety across the Rhine.

There was an odd witchcraft in that red beret. I remember we all crowded round just to touch it for luck, as if it were a talisman.

But Velp was a hospital above all things, the underground activities were additional—and incidental. As far as matron and the doctors

were concerned, the patients came first, the other responsibilities they accepted as well. . .

I never remember being miserable in Velp, even when things were grim.

One day in October the English dive-bombed some tanks in the main street of the town. Toot and I were on duty in the children's ward. We just heard one swooping scream and dived under the nearest cots.

When we noticed each other again we were both peering out with a baby under each arm.

The risks

That night the bombing was heavy and the guns were barking, and Mechteld, the laboratory assistant, with staring eyes dashed into my room. "I can't stand it," she screeched, literally tearing her hair. "If it doesn't stop I'll go raving mad . . ."

Two nurses had packed their bags and left the hospital without a word to anyone—because of the bombing—and I thought this was another case.

But it wasn't the war which was worrying Mechteld. It was Mendelsohn's Violin Concerto. Mr. Carritson used to come out at night and practise his violin in the emergency operating theatre under the lab. Apparently he was conscientious.

I laughed. Mendelsohn and Mr. Gerritson had succeeded where air raids, bombs and the Gestapo had failed, and it occurred to me that hysteria induced by the violin was one war risk we never thought we ran.

But there were other risks

TOMORROW
The Gestapo walk in . . .

justify it. The doctor and his wife cooked a wonderful meal, with venison from the bombed cold storage in the town (thanks to the boys). The nurses were escorted in to the dinner on the children's ward, where we ate by candlelight. Risky and crazy, but it happened. At night the boys continued to disappear. A band of men had come from Arnhem with the doctors. They slept in the children's ward during the day, and we never asked or knew where they went at night. Then one of them brought a red hat and a tin hat for a souvenir – the owner had just been smuggled across the Rhine.

There was an odd witchcraft about that beret. I remember we all crowded around it to touch it, as if it were a talisman. I never remember being miserable in Velp, even when things were grim. One day in October the English dive bombed some tanks in the main street of the town. Toot and I were on the children's ward. Remember hearing one swooping scream and we dived under the nearest cots. When we noticed each other again, we were both peering out with a baby under each arm. That night the bombing was very heavy, the guns were barking, and Mechteld, the laboratory assistant, with staring eyes, dashed into my room. 'I can't stand it', he screeched, 'if it doesn't stop I will go raving mad.' Two nurses had packed their bags and left the hospital, without a word to anyone, because of the bombing, I thought this was another case. But it wasn't the war that was the problem. It was Mendelssohn's Violin Concerto. Mr Gerritson used to come out at night and practise his violin in the emergency operating theatre under the laboratory. He was very conscientious. I laughed not ever thinking this could be a risk of the war that had succeeded where the bombs and the Gestapo had failed. But there were other risks. Little did we know that the Gestapo were going walk in.

My mother revisits the cemetery at Oosterbeek.

This must have been such a heartbreaking time – with thoughts of liberation raised and so near.

The staff were not to know that there would be another winter to survive, and, isolated in the hospital, they could not know of the dreadful deprivation that this winter would bring.

While the medical and nursing work continued and the clandestine resistance activity in the hospital increased, the 4th Lincolns had finally reached Holland.

CHAPTER ELEVEN

The 4th Lincolns are in Holland, winter 1944

My father wrote little of the time in the south of Holland, the period the Lincolns spent until they reached 'The Island', the area south of Arnhem, where they were to spend the winter of 1944.

'I am constantly hearing about the fine achievements of your battalion.' These were the words addressed to Lieutenant Colonel Peter Barclay by Field Marshall Montgomery when decorating him with the DSO he had won at Fontenay. High praise indeed as the Commander in Chief of the Allied Forces would not normally get to hear of the specific actions of individual battalions.

In fact, as this ceremony was taking place, the Lincolns had been placed under the direct command of the Canadians, and the objective of the Polar Bears was now the town of Rosendaal, some 20 miles away. Reading from *Saturday Night Soldiers* we see:

The Lincolns by now were 25% short of their full complement. Men were drafted in and the battalion began to lose much of its 'Lincolnshire' identity. D company was placed in 'Gorforce' and was left in reserve in the village of Baarle-Nassau area, still on the Belgian border, moving forward to the suburbs of the larger town of Breda after A, B and C companies had liberated the small villages en route to the town which was liberated at the end of October. On 2 November a ceremonial parade was held in Breda, where Dutch and allied flags were to be seen everywhere before the company rejoined the brigade at Rosendaal. From there the battalion advanced to the outskirts of Willemstad, a town on the southern bank of the River Maas estuary.

The German commander was asked to surrender, but refused, although did allow the several thousand Dutch civilians to be evacuated. My father would have felt the same emotions as my mother, in Arnhem, as the civilians with

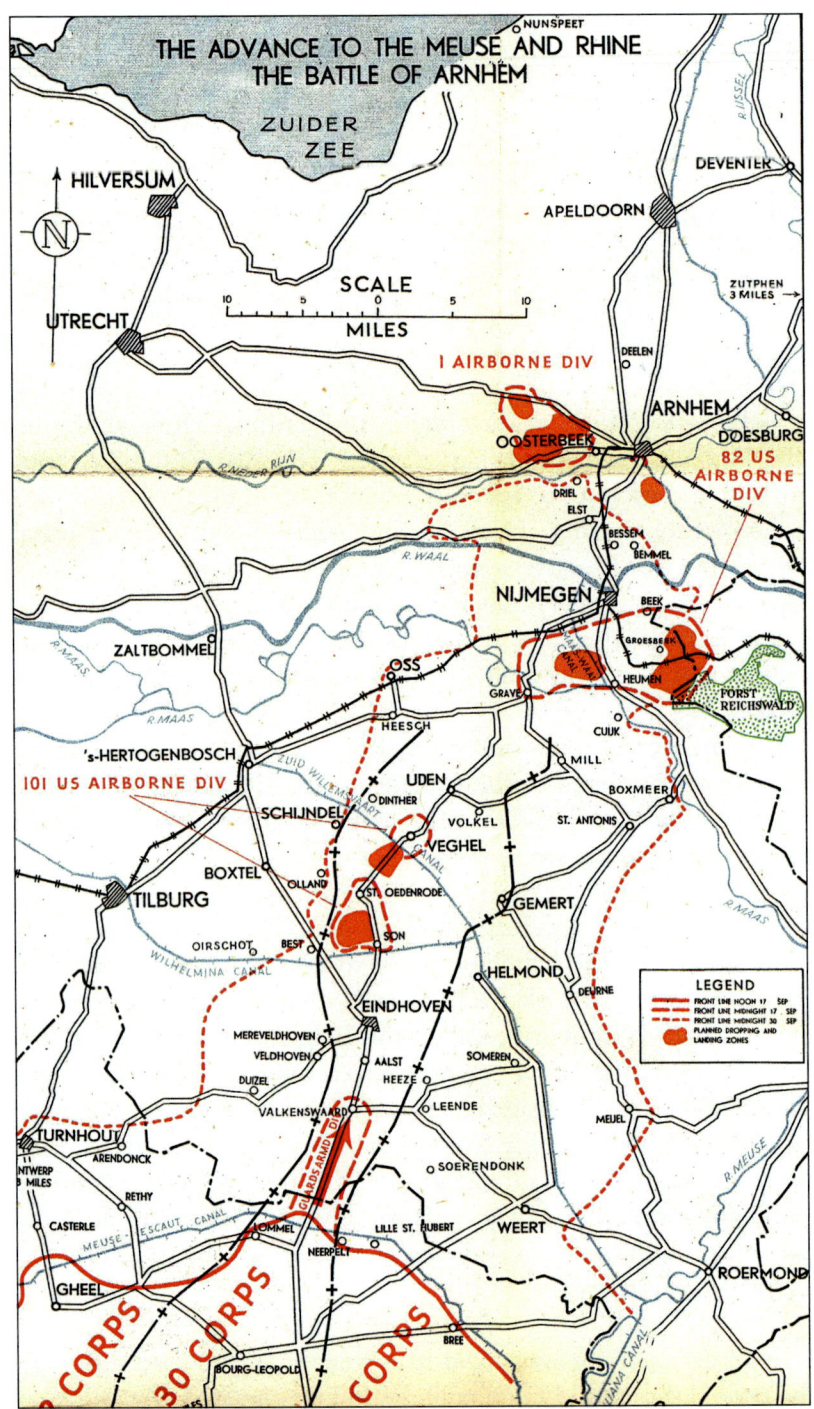

Turnhout to 'The Island'.

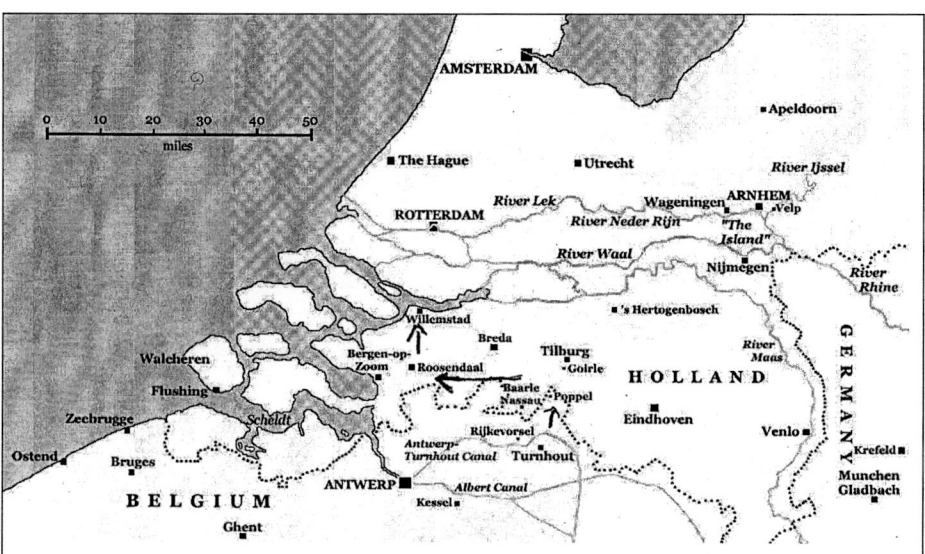

Northern Belgium and Southern Holland.

their few possessions passed by the ranks of soldiers. Willemstad was taken with no problems as the German forces had retreated at the time the civilian population was released.

During this spell of fighting, together with the Canadians and the Polish Armoured Division, might have been when my father recognised the bravery of the Polish troops. On one of the rare occasions he talked to me about the actual fighting, rather than simply giving a description of movements and locations, he described waiting in a wood by the side of a field that had probably been mined.

The Polish troops alongside the platoon had few words to say; when the decision to advance was made, they said 'we go'.

After this objective had been obtained, the Lincolns along with rest of the Polar Bears were now directed *back* south east to take position west of Venlo, near the Dutch German border, on the far east of Holland. This ceaseless manoeuvring must at times have seemed to be without clear purpose and reminds me of my father's words regarding the movements in Normandy:

At times … it was difficult to remember where you were, or even why.

The advance continued towards Venlo, just a few miles from the German border. It appears that the German positions were not well defended, and it was noted that the Dutch resistance were playing a prominent role in aiding the liberating forces. However, the Lincolns were not to move any further east to the German border, for on 29 November they were back on their way north west towards the city of Nijmegen, a large town on a section of land virtually surrounded by water.

The 4th Lincolns had been given the job of garrisoning 'The Island', only a few miles south of Arnhem.

In Velp, the hospital continued its medical work – in the increasingly dangerous climate following the failed airborne landings. The German occupying forces still sought to trace the Dutch resistance workers, and the Dutch Hunger Winter was about to begin.

CHAPTER TWELVE

Velp Hospital, November 1944

The Gestapo walk in and the Hunger Winter

Following the first Battle of Arnhem, the German troop activity escalated as they searched for Allied soldiers, either in hiding or as patients in the hospital. Life in the hospital became even more tense as the occupying German Forces began to suspect the hospital of being more than a place for the sick and injured. The entry at this time, from the book *Velp en de Oorlog 1940–1945* which, when translated, reads as follows:

27th November Strict identity controls, the hospital and the emergency hospital have been surrounded by Krauts. They are looking for wounded British soldiers. Futile. They completely missed the people in hiding (Onderduikers) – went right over their heads.

My mother's next newspaper article continues the story, telling more about that frightening time:

When the Germans raided the hospital the nurse on duty had to think fast to save her life and ours. The Gestapo were looking for wounded paratroopers; we knew they would not find any. An English nurse called Doris Langridge, the adopted daughter of a Dutch family, was on duty at the door. It was an apparently peaceful day in November and for once the guns were fairly quiet and the hospital calm. Doris saw the patrol and raised the alarm. Margot had the presence of mind to remember something which might have given us all away. She dashed into the children's ward and swept up all the ashtrays in the tablecloth and stuffed them in the linen basket. Children don't smoke.

I began to realise anger is stronger than fear. We hated the indignity the search involved, we forgot to be afraid, the Germans were all over the hospital, but they were not quick enough. The show they missed was like a slapstick comedy, but not funny. Mr Bernard shot into bed in the private patients' ward, and tried to look ill. Mr Gerritson, Joop and the rest ran straight through the panel in Fenna's room, and hid in the hole in the roof. One of the doctors spoke to the Germans with his back to the curtain which covered the panel. The Gestapo were too afraid to go through to the fever ward, which was lucky as that is where the radio was hidden.

Wolter was the one who did not get away and became an emergency case. The trolley was wheeled into the operating room, the house surgeon and the theatre sister scrubbed up calmly and Wolter had his appendix out. The Germans went away. Later, remembering it with Fenna, I said how amazed I was how calm the staff had been. 'Don't you believe it,' she said, 'we were all scared stiff'. But it did not show.

Woman of Arnhem—4. The day the doctor operated on a fit man... to save his life!

WHEN the Germans raided the hospital, the nurse on duty had to think fast to save her life and ours.

The Gestapo were looking for wounded paratroopers. We knew they wouldn't find any in Velp, but there was a lot we didn't want them to discover . . .

An English nurse called Doris Langridge, the adopted daughter of a Dutch family, was on duty at the door. It was her job to take messages, answer the telephone, and keep track of all visitors—including the enemy!

It was an apparently peaceful day in November. For once the guns were fairly quiet and the hospital was calm. It was still calm, in a hectic sort of way, 'two seconds after Doris saw the patrol and gave the alarm.

Margot had the presence of mind to remember something which might have given us all away. She dashed into the children's ward, swept up the ashtrays with the tablecloth and stuffed the lot in a dirty linen basket. Children don't smoke.

After that she went back to the ward, and wondered what the thermometer would register if she took her own temperature instead of the patients' . . .

I began to realise that anger is stronger than fear. We hated the indignity the search involved and we forgot to be afraid. The Germans seemed to be all over the hospital all at once, and we despised them for being there . . .

But they weren't quite quick enough. The show they missed was like a slapstick comedy, but not funny.

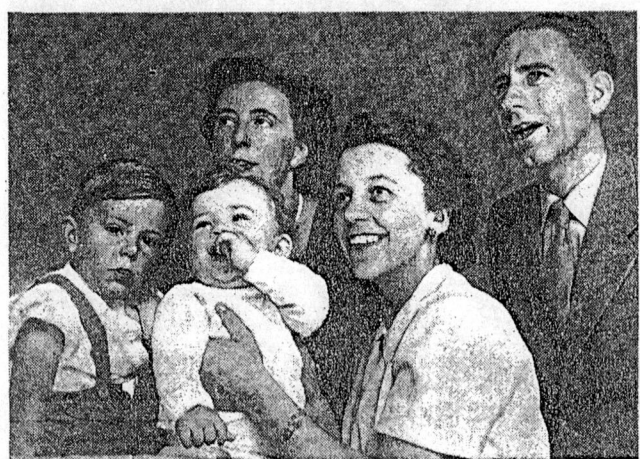

Twelve years ago Wolter hid on the operating table and as Germans searched the doctor took out his perfectly sound appendix. In our picture the author (second from the right) meets Wolter and his family in a happy reunion.

The Gestapo walk in . . .

Nies Cartwright-Rutgers continues her story of Arnhem

takes for granted, like the next breath.

We took it for granted the night the operating theatre was practically disintegrating around us.

The Gestapo walk in.

It did show the day Pastor Schaars was sent to Dachau. He was considered a dangerous subversive element, but to the people of Velp was a loved and trusted friend. He was not operating from within the hospital, but was the spider in the middle of the web, a man who knew everything and everybody. We all knew what Gestapo could do, and that they would try hard to persuade the pastor to talk. Those days after the arrest the hospital seemed to die, we felt frozen with fear. At those times, if we had any off duty periods we should have had nowhere to go, the roads were not safe and the British were carrying out a non-stop blitz. Yet we never doubted we could endure, we never thought about it. One night the operating theatre was almost disintegrating around us. The only thing that seemed steady were the eyes and hands of the surgeon. The instruments trembled and the walls shook, the 18 carbide lamps, the only light we had, hissed and flickered around the table. Many lives were in danger, but at that moment there was one life in that little circle of light that was being saved, it was as simple as that.

My mother talks of these events so calmly in her summary; the story of the operating by carbide emergency light is described in the book *Velp en de Oorlog 1940–1945*, which cousin Annelies, living in Velp, was able to obtain for me.

Pastor Schaars must have been an important figurehead for the community. This is the only reference to him I have come across, but clearly his survival after the horrors of Dachau led to great joy.

Away from the hospital, the winter of starvation, the 'Hongerwinter' had started. The Dutch population were starving. The story of Anne Frank and the deportation of Holland's Jewish population to concentration camps is well known, but relatively little has been written about the Dutch famine of 1944–45 when the Dutch civilians were literally starving.

The failure of the Allied Forces to cross the Rhine at Arnhem in September 1945 meant only a small slice of south-west Holland had been liberated. The major cities – Amsterdam, Rotterdam and the Hague – remained under German occupation until the end of the war. Although the Allied forces periodically launched attacks, it was, sadly, simply not a priority. The Allies had crossed the Siegfried Line in Belgium and France, pushed eastwards into Germany and left a large contingent of German soldiers effectively cut off. Holland had already been ransacked, factories dismantled and thousands of people moved from the coastal towns inland. The Dutch had been led to believe in the early autumn of 1944, that liberation by the Allied forces was imminent, partly because of the Market Garden operation in September

Pastor Schaars after his release from Dachau.

(which failed so disastrously) and partly as a result of misinformation heard on Radio Oranje. Clearly the Nazi occupying forces also believed this and in anticipation of invasion, large swathes of the countryside were flooded, including valuable and productive polders (reclaimed land). The ports of Rotterdam and Amsterdam suffered great destruction, increasing the difficulty of transporting food supplies by sea. Hundreds of thousands of Dutch men between the ages of 18 and 50 were forcibly shipped to Germany to support the war effort, and since June 1942 there had been the continuing deportation of Dutch Jews to the concentration camps to meet their death. Out of the 140,000 pre-war Jewish population, 105,000 were found and murdered – a higher proportion than any other western European country. As well as these destructive acts, from October onwards policies were introduced to procure from the Dutch items such as blankets, clothing, radios and bicycles. The export of foodstuffs, cattle and machinery to Germany continued at great cost.

An added problem was created by the Allied bombardment and air assaults on cities. Nijmegen, the city my father would pass through in the autumn of 1944, had been heavily hit, with hundreds of civilians dead, a high price to pay for a liberation that was still some way off. As winter closed in on some three million people, fears of a national tragedy grew.

The Dutch Prime Minister Pieter Gerbrandy and Winston Churchill had met at Downing Street on 5 October. It was a difficult meeting. The latter was told that the Germans were no longer feeding the Dutch and were looting Holland's food supplies. The suggestion by the Swedish Red Cross that they might supply food was not acceptable because 'it would only feed the Germans' and exacerbate the problem.

By November 1944 the average calorie intake for an adult had dropped to 900 calories. The trips to the farms and countryside were becoming more difficult to undertake and even fewer bicycles for transport were available. The civilian population reverted to primitive forms of bartering, as cutlery, clothing and tools were exchanged for food. Stories of humiliation, shame and begging were as common as acts of kindness by those in possession of food. The misery persisted, albeit with continued pressure by the exiled Dutch Government and royalty on Allied leaders and neutral countries (Sweden and Switzerland) to address the situation. Eventually there was a small shipment in January 1945, transported on the canal system to the major cities from the north east of Holland. This helped morale, but was not sufficient. Queen Wilhelmina wrote to Churchill and Eisenhower in January. It was reported the average food intake for adults now supplied

Food at last – temporary relief. Food kitchens kept many people from starving to death.

The results of starvation. The child on the left has rickets.

only 500 to 800 calories a day for those trapped in occupied Holland. Finally, under pressure from Montgomery and others, Eisenhower, the Supreme Commander, agreed to take action and the food situation in *liberated* Holland improved, but not in areas north of the Maas, Waal and Rhine, which of course included Arnhem. The threat posed by the food crisis was now not only humanitarian. The Dutch were increasingly bitter that the generosity shown after the end of the First World War to German and Austrian refugee children was being repaid by these savage policies. There was silence in the cities as traffic stopped and the starving kept still as a blanket of snow covered the ground. Sugar beet and tulip bulbs were becoming staple foods and sickness and medical conditions became worse. The political dimension was that the Dutch populace was in part becoming radicalised. They may have hated the Germans, but feelings towards the Allies had become less warm as a sense of abandonment increased, and there was intelligence available that indicated the growth of communist sympathies in the east of the country. While the Allied Command dithered, thousands of Dutch civilians died of starvation.

The staff and patients at the hospital in Velp were more fortunate. Being in the east of the country there were farms that could be reached, although comments at the time, translated from the book *Velp in de Oorlog* note:

Rich and poor with cart and try for money or kind words in order to get some food. The farms are visited by hundreds of people every day, not only from Velp but also from far out west – Utrecht, Rotterdam and the Hague, people on foot, desperate for food, on foot looking for food, driven by hunger. Not a night goes by without the Bishop Staal School, the catholic boys' school on Nieustraat, now used as a refuge, hosting travellers. They find a bed and something to eat. The next day the same thing 'Do you have some rye for me perhaps, can you spare me some potatoes we don't have any more,' they would say. There are farmers with a heart of gold, but some whose wallets are stuffed full of gold. Their linen closets are bulging. They demanded gold or the sack of grain stays closed. The bread ration was reduced again to 1600 grams for 14 days – you can't do much with that. On the 14th December supplies of milk amounted to 90 litres. Supplemented by powdered milk, the supply for children and sick patients was limited to half a litre a day. The stove in the hospital has been lit. Stacks of pancakes are made. There is never a hungry soul in there. There is a lot of bread for the patients.

As my mother said in her newspaper article, there was always enough food in the hospital. *'You could always rely on the boys; one night they came back with wine and venison from a bombed out house in Arnhem.'*

To add to the misery was the uncertainty about how long this could continue. False hopes and rumours continued despite the devastating failed attack on Arnhem in September and again taken from the book *Velp en de Oorlog* we note:

Already from the Betuwe 'the Island' you can hear the incessant thud of the artillery.

The besieged and trapped starving people in Arnhem were not to know the Allies were unable to move from the Island.

The severe winter had made conditions even more miserable for the 4th Lincolns stuck on the Island, the flat low-lying area south of the River Rhine, waiting for the time to come when they could advance again further into occupied Holland.

CHAPTER THIRTEEN

The Nijmegen Home Guard, December 1944 – March 1945

The 4th Lincolns on the Island

Just inside Holland, the Rhine divides into two branches. The Nederrijn flows north west to join the Ijssel at Arnhem, while the southern branch of the Rhine flows west past Nijmegen and becomes known as the River Waal. In between these rivers is the area known as the Island. It is desolate, low lying and prone to flooding. The Romans called it the 'Island of the Batavians', the latter being the original inhabitants of that country. After heavy fighting in

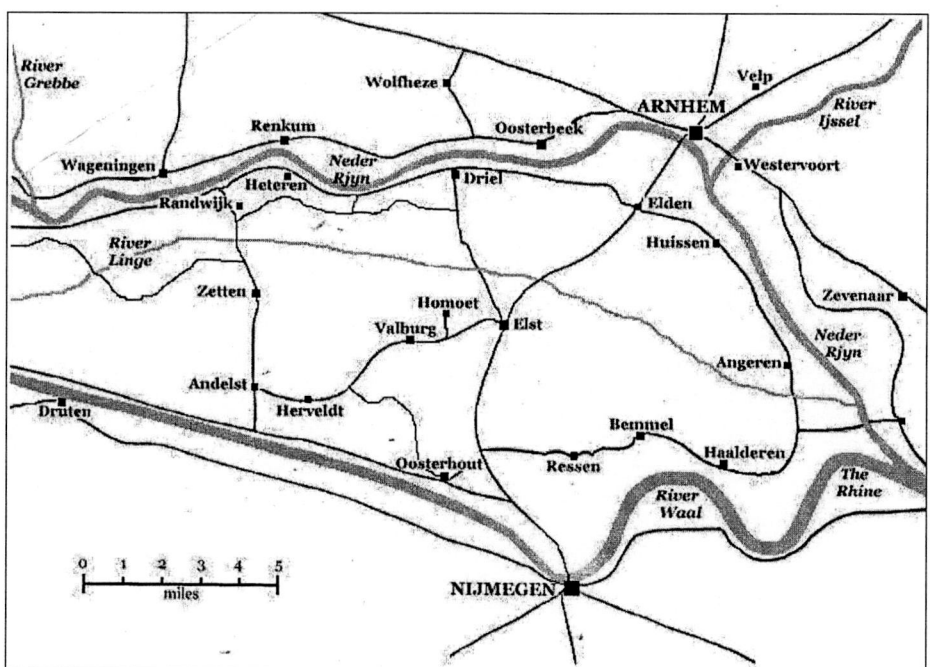

The Island.

the failed attempt to reach Arnhem, the wreckage of military hardware was everywhere, houses were damaged and many reinforced with sandbags. No trenches could be built to hide from shelling. The Allies had moved back from the villages on the south bank of the Nederrijn, to avoid the forward troops becoming isolated, and the Germans had reoccupied these villages. So both sets of troops occupied what was effectively 'No Man's Water' since the whole area was flooded after the Germans blew up the dykes on the bank of the Nederrijn. The map on page 85 illustrates the situation and photographs of the countryside illustrate the devastating flooding.

The Lincolns arrived in the area known as the Island in December 1944 but the final offensive to take and liberate Arnhem would not take place until the spring of the following year. After the relative comfort of Nijmegen, the Lincolns crossed the Waal to reach Ressen, a small town a few miles north of the river. The area was flooded and the troops had to rely on flat-bottomed canvas-sided boats for transport.

My father describes his time on the Island in only two sentences:

We spent the winter months on the Island, between Nijmegen and Arnhem, living in a deserted farm. Sleeping on the floor was a luxury but lone night guard in a pitch black barn was not.

Much of the land was flooded.

The 4th Lincolns on boat patrol.

It was a curious lull for the battalion, for although there was some fighting during the several months spent on the Island, no large territorial advance was made. It was just as miserable for the enemy, with mud everywhere and the small roads, in between flooded areas, littered with the debris of war from the failed first Arnhem attack in September.

A stalemate had been reached on both the Western and Eastern fronts. However, Hitler reminded his generals that he still held more territory than at the beginning of the war. The German defensive victory at Arnhem had increased their morale and of course prolonged the war into 1945. The Luftwaffe still had a large fighter capability (although lacking petrol and supplies) and the army had been reinforced by lowering the call-up age to 16. Hitler decided on a plan to strike back into Belgium towards Antwerp. This was the 'Battle of the Bulge', which started on 16 December 1944, the last ditch attempt to split the allied forces in two as they continued their drive into Germany. Fierce fighting by the American forces, led by General Patton, resisted the attack, and Hitler's last desperate gamble failed.

Bogged down on the Island the boring wet miserable routine of the 4th Lincolns continued. Some of the British soldiers were allowed home on ten days' leave. It seems my father was not one of the lucky ones, since I am sure he would have entered it into his account. The Polar Bears had some local skirmishes with the enemy, and they were reviewed on a visit from Montgomery. On 12 March they were relieved by the 2nd Essex, moved to a reserve area where there was some dry land and prepared to leave the Island.

The plan for the 49th Division was to set out to capture the villages between Nijmegen and Arnhem. They moved east through the village of Angeren towards the bank of the Nederrijn. There was German resistance and although it was sporadic and chaotic, there were sadly further casualties, and more wounded. The Nederrijn was crossed with no opposition, and by 10 April the Lincolns were located at Zevenaar, six miles south east of Arnhem. As a result of high-quality intelligence from within the town of Arnhem, it became known that there was a Dutch SS regiment there. Many mines and booby traps had been laid within the town. On the morning of 13 April, the Lincolns had assembled at Westervoort, on the south bank of the River Ijssel, a few miles south of the small town of Velp.

The second Battle of Arnhem was about to begin.

CHAPTER FOURTEEN

Velp Hospital, spring 1945

'Through the wreckage to happiness'

The final article in the series that my mother wrote for the newspaper series told of the relief and joy as the second Battle of Arnhem was won by the Allies and the liberation of Velp came at last.

> The night Louisa put the bomb under the rose bush I knew nothing on earth could ruffle Matron … We'd just finished boiling the water for the babies' morning baths. That was a nightly ritual because we had no electricity. We used to heat the water over the stove and put it in great pans which were wrapped in blankets so that it would keep moderately warm until the morning. … The patients needed settling, and I was planning to do some work for the exams which had been put back until December.

Through the wreckage to happiness

WOMAN OF ARNHEM

Nies Cartwright-Rutgers ends her story

THE night Louisa put the bomb under the rose bush I knew nothing on earth could ruffle matron . . . It was a noisy night above the ground, and busy down below in the cellars of the hospital which had become the women's and children's ward.

We'd just finished boiling the water for the babies' morning baths. That was a nightly ritual because of the lack of electricity. We used to heat the water over the stove and put it in great pans which were wrapped in blankets so that it would keep moderately warm until the morning. We couldn't afford to keep the stoves alight all night.

'Through the wreckage to happiness' – my mother's final article.

I can hear it now – thump, thump, I was in the throes of 'blood circulation chapter three' when it came bouncing down the stairs. Nobody screamed, nobody moved. Louisa, a big bonnie girl with a ponderous walk marched across to the bomb, tucked it under her arm like a baby and walked upstairs.

'What have you done with it girl', asked the matron. 'I've put it under the rose bush', she replied, 'the one in the far corner'. Nobody had hysterics, because nobody felt hysterical. This was the effect that matron and the house surgeon had. There must have been many moments like this, but nothing was frightening when they were around.

I remember one day Margot came back, bubbling over with excitement. She tore back into the hospital chattering about – Blackpool ! Jan, her fiancé, had taken her to some English paratroopers who were hidden in a barn. One was from Blackpool and Margot's sister had married a Blackpool man, so she claimed a sort of proprietary right to the town. We told her any Englishman would tell her he was from Blackpool if he thought this would please a pretty Dutch nurse.

Harold Riley was the paratrooper referred to. He came from Lytham St Annes in Lancashire and there is a paragraph in this final article where he tells something of his story.

'A Paratrooper's Postscript' is the heading given to the short account by Harold Riley:

I met Jan five weeks after the first Battle of Arnhem. I was riding along on a large bicycle behind an underground worker, a Dutch policeman, we passed several German soldiers, and one of them made to intercept us. Jan beckoned us on to allay any suspicion, and from there shepherded us in our escape. To tell the story of those nightmare months after the battle would take a book. I had set out with a friend from a church where we had made one of our last fighting stands. We went through the town of Arnhem, and were stopped five times by Germans on the way. Eventually Jan took us to a house in Velp, where we met his fiancée. That was Margot. We planned our getaway. I walked through the town with Margot on my arm. And I wasn't the first 'English boy friend' who might have sent her to a concentration camp or death. The underground organisation at Velp provided us with papers and a passport to freedom. Jan and another of the boys drove us in a Red Cross van to a refuge from where we could escape. With their help finally we drifted in a rowing boat down the River Waal to freedom. They and others like them had risked their lives to help us. I will never forget them.

Another book found in my parents' collection, which confirms these acts of bravery and heroism, is titled *Herinneringen aan de Bevrijding van Velp* (Memories of the Liberation of Velp). This book was published in February 2006, to commemorate the date of 16 April 1945 and the 60 years of freedom from occupation. It describes briefly the liberation by the 49th West Riding Division – the Polar Bears – with many photographs of the action in the town at that time, as well as several personal accounts. On page 107, under the section 'Organised Group Resistance', the writing describes at least four active resistance groups by the end

A joyful reunion with Margot.

of 1941. Working with these was the hospital in Velp, 'Het Velpse Ziekenhuis', where my mother trained and worked. I have translated the section:

> Velp Hospital was not only an important hiding place for the Jewish population, but also for members of the resistance, paratroopers and other escaped allies. Its members secretly looked for food, for example, for the political prisoners in the Rotterdamsche Bank. Food was smuggled, and the 'onderduikers' or underdivers (those hidden) dressed as nursing assistants (in Het Wit) meaning, literally, dressed in white, transported 15 escaped prisoners to a safe place nearby and from there into the country. The 'centre of illegal activity' was the name the Germans gave to the hospital. It has in vain often been raided.

On the preceding page are written several 'Individual Verzet' or acts of individual heroism, some with a tragic ending, and one of which reads:

> In the hetzevelde booklet is recorded that a Velp resistance worker helped a Jewish lady and her daughter safely from the hospital in the funeral car of the firm Van Middelkoop to a family in Rozendaal Avenue. Sadly both were deported to Auschwitz later.

The staff and 'Underdivers' in front of the hospital.

As the spring of 1945 unfolded, the Dutch civilian population of Velp knew the end of the war must be near. The Rhine had been crossed in four places in Germany (north and south of the town of Wesel, south east of Arnhem). General Patton crossed the Rhine on 22 March, just before midnight, and the Americans had beaten the British in the race to cross the river. Churchill crossed the Rhine in a Landing Craft Mechanised (LCM) on 24 March. He then went to the railway bridge at Wesel, on the front line, later criticised by Eisenhower as far too dangerous. During that time before the liberation, which my mother describes as a strange and violent time, the hospital was increasingly busy with wounded civilians as the bombing of Arnhem and the surrounding area continued.

The liberation of Velp was imminent, but with this came the increased dangers associated with the heavy fighting. More entries in the book describe the situation and by the end of the second week of April, with liberation so close, the civilian population became increasingly tense. I translate from the text of the book *Velp en de Oorlog*:

Friday 13 April: 'Where are the Tommies now? Is it a moment for people to emerge from the cellar? Water supplies must be refilled. Velp looks shabby: stone, sand, ruins and shot up tree branches lie in the street. Burnt out houses, houses with no more glass. Dare we light the stove? The shelling starts again. The explosions seem to be heavier than last night. At half past two it peaks then it slows down until it is silent again. The hospital has not been hit yet, but three grenades were thrown into a sitting room and the window panes have been shot out. Wounded are still being brought in, and to make more places patients are lying on mattresses under the beds…

Friday evening: The rumours that Roosevelt has died of a stroke are persistent. A bridgehead must have been formed at the head of the Ijssel. The Allies could be here in an instant. All over Velp the Jerries have cut down trees. The artillery continues to fire.

But it would not be long before the hospital was hit.

In the evening around 9 pm Velp was hit by several volleys from a night fighter. Two heavily wounded individuals were taken to the Velp Hospital. The hospital has increasingly the look of a field hospital. In practice all patients are in fact war wounded. The hospital received many hits on its upper level. The lift fell down with a thunderous roar after a pulley cable was torn apart by a shell. The 'Tommies' were advancing: on the Arnhem side of the town you can hear the rattle of machine guns.

Somehow news was getting through to the people of Velp. On 12 April President Roosevelt had indeed suffered a stroke, while in Warm Springs, Georgia, where he had been staying to try to rest and recuperate. He died within minutes of a massive cerebral haemorrhage.

I will let my mother take up the story of life in Velp in those final days, with the continuation of the rest of the last article. She wrote:

Life had a strange and violent pattern those last few weeks before liberation, but the hospital imposed its own discipline. The women's wards were crowded with mattresses on the floor and we slept when and where we could. My usual spot was under a bed in the men's ward. What would you say, said the patient, if you met me after the war and I introduce you as the girl who slept under my bed for weeks! There was a constant noise of guns and bombs in the background, to the extent that silence would have shocked us. But then came the wonderful day when the tanks rumbled through Velp. They were British tanks, the language we heard was English and the war was to be over. We gave a terrific concert and a pale wisp of a girl who used to help the doctors played a supporting role. I didn't know her name then. Now she is called Audrey Hepburn.

Audrey Hepburn in an early photograph, as my mother would have known her.
© Pictorial Press Ltd/Alamy.

Audrey Hepburn was born Audrey Kathleen Ruston, in Brussels, Belgium, but lived in Arnhem during her childhood and the war years. In later life she found fame both as an actress in theatre, playing the lead character in *Gigi*, on Broadway, and in film, most notably in *Breakfast at Tiffany's*. Her father, Joseph Ruston, was English, and between 1935 and 1938 she attended a boarding school for girls, in Eltham, Kent. In 1935 her parents divorced, and her father, a Nazi sympathiser, left the family. In 1939 her mother, Ella, moved the family back to the Netherlands, to Arnhem, believing it would be safe from German attack. After the German invasion in 1940 Ella assumed the name Edda van Heemstra, believing her own English sounding name was too dangerous. By 1944 Audrey had become a proficient ballerina, and secretly danced for groups of people to raise money for the Dutch Resistance. She suffered as many did in the starvation winter of 1945 and subsequently developed anaemia and respiratory problems. She witnessed atrocities – her uncle and mother's cousin were shot in front of her, for belonging to the Dutch Resistance. She records how she felt permanently traumatised by the events witnessed, and these events led her to become involved with UNICEF later

Sergeant Cartwright (centre), sleeves rolled up.

in life. After her final film role she increased her involvement with UNICEF and in 1988 visited Ethiopia, Turkey and South America, continuing to make visits until September 1992, only four months before she died from bowel cancer.

Liberation for Arnhem and Velp had come at last, recorded not only by my mother in her newspaper account, but also in the third page of her letter to my niece Amy:

> After the paratroop landings in nearby Ooosterbeek and the subsequent fighting and evacuation of Arnhem we were left in a sort of no man's land. The English Army were first across the Rhine, now and then they let us know they were there, by the odd shell or two! Then on the 16th April 1945, after a fortnight heavy fighting, when we had to take refuge in the cellars, with the women and children, the English tanks rolled in and we were liberated! The first visit we had was from the Canadian Medical Corps, who provided us with everything we were short of. The most important thing was penicillin. We could have saved so many lives if we had had that. Shell wounds and lacerations used to fester and cause blood poisoning.

Herinneringen aan de Bevrijding van Velp

16 April 1945

gefotografeerd en

beschreven

Liberation at last.

German troops surrender in Velp.

The nurses cheer (my mother is front row, third from the left). Little did she know that coming with the tanks was the soldier she was about to meet, then marry and spend the rest of her life with, a marriage that would last 65 years.

The liberation was also celebrated by the newspaper of the town, the *Velpsche Courant*. Somehow an edition was printed on 16 April 1945, with the title 'First emergency edition after the Liberation' and I have translated the first sentence:

'Bevrijding' Na een bangen smart-tijd klonk heden morgen de haart kreet. VRIJ! De Engelsche stridjkrachten trokken ons dorp binnenonde de daven vanonze juichkreten

'Liberation'. After a difficult painful period the heartfelt cry rings out this morning. FREE! English forces entered our town under the cacophony of our cheers.

The description of the liberation was the final paragraph in the last of the newspaper articles my mother wrote, and these were the words again, with which the articles concluded:

Then came that wonderful day when the tanks rumbled through Velp, they were British tanks, the language we heard English and the war was over for us.

CHAPTER FIFTEEN

'You have come back', Arnhem April 1945

The Lincolns and the taking of Arnhem, April 1945

Finally that spring we moved forward to what would be our last action, taking part in the liberation of Arnhem, which is where I believe Skip was wounded.

This is how my father began the last part of the account of his wartime experiences. The Lincolns set off for the south-eastern approach to Arnhem on the morning of 13 April 1945. Resistance was encountered, there was further fighting and the intelligence that had been gathered, indicating weakened German forces, was not accurate. The Lincolns had been

The 49th cross the Rhine.

engaged in a battle to take a huge factory that appeared to be full of German troops. It transpired this was one of the key points for the defence of Arnhem. Although the intelligence obtained had indicated that there were fewer than a thousand troops in Arnhem, in fact more than 1,600 German soldiers were taken prisoner; clearly the forces were greater in number than anticipated. There were 62 British soldiers killed. The following day, on 14 April, the Lincolns 'mopped up' between Rosendaal and Velp and my father describes it as follows:

> The action was successful. We eventually took up position in the garden of a house which had evidently been the headquarters of a Nazi command. The walls were decorated with pictures. Arthur Gill had fun putting a bullet though each one. We moved forward to an attractive village called Velp – and you know what happened from there. Someone came over to our billet and asked if I would play the piano, there was a little party involving some nurses. From that point your mum and I were in constant touch, by letter or visits from Germany.

In fact, we had to get my parents to clarify the circumstances of their meeting. It was in a semi-shelled house, and there was an intact piano that my father started to play. The music was 'Begin the Beguine', a song written by

Scenes of destruction after the battle.

Cole Porter in 1935 that became very popular dance music in the 1940s. This was the music my mother referred to, and the music she requested be played at her funeral service 67 years later.

The date of the meeting was 17 April 1945, and the final paragraph of the last article that she wrote for the newspaper reads as follows:

> Finally, we knew that we would be freed. After the fighting ceased, the matron gave us permission to go out, the town was coming back to life again, we walked though streets where it was safe at last to shine a light.
>
> From one deserted house where the French windows had been blown away there was a piano, and an English soldier was playing a song titled 'Begin the Beguine'. And it is the music I shall love all my life for I married the man who played it.

The joy and euphoria was of course not shared by every Dutch citizen. There had been a significant degree of collaboration with the enemy, and Velp was no exception. The derogatory term for the women who had collaborated with the Nazis was 'Moffenmeiden', and they were soon pitilessly gathered together and marched away to an uncertain future.

The second attack on Arnhem had been successful. A huge price had been paid in both operations. One of the most moving short accounts was recorded by Matthew Halton, a war correspondent for the American CBC. He describes how he followed the troops across the river and in his words:

> ...felt it was appropriate that a British Division, the 49th, should take Arnhem at long last, and write the words 'Paid in Full' across another chapter of British history. Last September the world stopped breathing to watch this town. If the British Army had been able to link hands with the British airborne forces that had landed at Arnhem and Oosterbeek, the Rhine would have been crossed then, and the course of the war turned, as armoured divisions would be poured into Hanover and Westphalia.

That of course did not happen.

Robert Dunnett, a war correspondent for the BBC, also covered the Second Battle of Arnhem, arriving on 17 April. He described the desolation and the sight of the city still burning. There is another account of the same story, so it is difficult to know how to attribute the tale. In the book *The Polar Bears: Monty's Left Flank*, there is a quote attributed to Dunnett, recorded at the time of his visit on 17 April:

A lone Dutchman, the first civilian we had encountered, came slowly down a long street. He shook hands. 'You have come back' he said quietly. Just that. The British had come back, as they always do.

The Canadian forces played a huge role in the action. My parents kept, along with all their records, cuttings and photographs, a copy of Norman Phillips' book *Holland and the Canadians*. The introduction by the president of the Canadian Netherlands committee pays tribute to the forces of the British Empire, and describes how the book would be a gift to express the admiration and gratitude of the Dutch population.

It shows a picture of the country before liberation, and the photographs graphically, and sometimes harrowingly, show the faces of destruction and results of the winter of starvation, as well as the joyous scenes at the time of liberation. I noted above that the 49th Division had come under the command of the Canadian forces. The part of the account in the book covering the liberation of Arnhem describes how the 49th Division were battling for Arnhem. It was a deserted town, the civilian population, over 150,000, evacuated, great trees felled for use as barriers and the empty half destroyed, looted houses fought for one by one.

As the push towards the German border in the east of Holland continued, a priority became the need to feed the Dutch, or those who had survived the awful 'Hongerwinter'. The gruesome actions perpetrated by the occupying German forces was the policy of vengeance against the Dutch population. Deliberate starvation left a desperate and hungry population at times surviving on beets and tulip bulbs. The supplies that had previously been agreed to by Prime Ministers Churchill of Britain and Gerbrandy of the Netherlands earlier in the year, and sent by airborne drop, had long since gone. The remaining German command, the last on Netherlands soil, had retreated into 'Fortress Holland', an area between the Ijsselmeer to the north with the great rivers of the Rhine and Maas to the south and bounded on the east by the water barrier of the 'Grebbe Line'. A strange series of talks took place between representatives of the liberating allied forces and the Germans on the last few days of April. Allied air activity over Fortress Holland ceased by agreement of both sides. Finally, an odd truce had been negotiated, with great difficulty, and at last the stockpiled food could be delivered to the starving population. The truce negotiated to allow the delivery of supplies to the starving population had required involvement of the highest order, for although the war was essentially lost the German command would not surrender, only agree to a truce, threatening wholesale destruction of further cities and towns in western Holland if this was not agreed to. The German command was led by the Nazi Reichskommissar Arthur Seyss-Inquart. The Allied forces had been wedded to the idea of unconditional surrender for years, but humanitarian reasons finally prevailed for the moment. The startling advance west from Arnhem had pushed the German forces back to the Grebbe Line, but it was halted and negotiations continued to allow for the passage of food convoys to north west Holland. The advancing troops were told of the impending truce. The threat from Seyss-Inquart to open the sea dykes and flood the countryside meant any allied force movements against the German opposition would be followed by court-martial. At the end of April the food convoys poured through the Polar Bear lines and the troops became involved in the effort to feed the starving Dutch population trapped in the west, particularly Amsterdam.

The operations to feed the starving Dutch were named Manna (the RAF operation) and Chowhound (the US Army/Airforce operation). In the digital and technological age we live in it is now possible to see aerial film of the operation on the internet.

On the morning of 29 April, a Sunday, the Allied air forces started to drop hundreds of tons of supplies on four designated drop zones, and the relief would at last begin to have an effect. Although substantial food delivery could be achieved by the drop, the collection and distribution of the food could take up to two weeks, as bridges had been destroyed and not one streetcar, tram or electric train was left in Holland. The starving Dutch spelled out 'Thank You' in rocks in the tulip fields.

The final liberation of the west of Holland was near. Hitler committed suicide on 30 April; the surrender of the German forces imminent. It is astonishing to think that my father was at the very town where it happened, Wageningen, a few miles west of Arnhem and he wrote as follows:

> We had become used to the excited civilians and even more so when whilst we were at Wageningen all the German forces in Holland surrendered.

At 4.00 p.m., 3 May, in the Hotel de Wereld, in the shattered town of Wageningen, General Johannes Blaskowicz, the German Commander in Chief in the Netherlands surrendered to the Canadian General Charles Foulkes, and General Eisenhower's Chief of Staff (Lieutenant General Bedell-Smith), in the presence of Prince Bernhard of the Netherlands. The war in Holland was over and a BBC mobile recording van was present to record the event. On the evening of 4 May came the news that all German troops in north-west Germany, Denmark and Western Holland had surrendered unconditionally to take effect from 8.00 a.m. on the morning of 5 May.

My father was in Wageningen when the surrender was signed.

Blaskowitz finally signed the document having 'needed 24 hours to study it' on the morning of 6 May – more than 24 hours after fighting ceased.

Two days later, on 7 May, the Polar Bears, having moved west, entered the city of Utrecht. Passing through ranks of fully armed German soldiers was a tense situation, but the German forces fulfilled the surrender conditions as ordered and the only impediment was the mass of wildly cheering crowds. My father wrote:

> Nothing compared to the reception at Utrecht when thousands of Dutch people greeted us as we entered. It was difficult to move through and all the vehicles were swarming with well wishers, mostly young girls, on board.

In a separate letter, dated 8 May, VE Day, sent to my grandparents, my father describes again the reception in Utrecht. It is a very touching letter, one which I had not realised existed and which I found exceptionally moving.

Utrecht as my father describes it.

It reads as follows:

My Dear Mother, Dad and Barry,

At last!! What a day to be writing to you. I can hardly believe that it is true, but anyway, it is to be announced today by Churchill. I'll bet you are happy and were last night. Anyway here I am quite safe and well and Lofty and Lolly are also OK. I expect you have been wondering where I am and if I am alright. I don't suppose it matters now but I can tell you I am still in Holland, after the battle of Arnhem. We did not have too bad a time, liberated one or two small places and stayed for a time at A LOVELY LITTLE PLACE CALLED VELP WHERE LIVED THOSE FRIENDS OF WHOM I TOLD YOU. (My capitals) Then we moved but there was little doing of course, the Germans were beginning to crack up, then came the great news, of the surrender in N. Germany.

Yesterday was a great day, we moved into Utrecht. Did those people go wild! And the news that all the Germans had finished! The Battalion had to march in single file through the streets they were so packed and the carriers in which we were riding looked like carnival wagons, at one time we had about a dozen civvies on board. All the day this went on, the band was out and hundreds of civvies dancing in the streets – they kept coming to the building where we were, dancing and cheering. Today we are free of course and I will be going to have a look at the city – Utrecht is a very big place as you know. I suppose they will be celebrating, although the poor devils have little to celebrate with. Yesterday great aircraft were swooping over the city dropping stuff I suppose. And the strange sight of Jerries, marching or driving in carts through the town to the surrender areas – looking pretty well down and out, but, some of them not unhappy. We are all wondering what it will be like in England (I do hope Mr Cartwright doesn't get too much beer). I am very pleased to think how relieved you must be and relieved to think it is over. But it has been a terrible time, and the victory can bring little comfort to the people such as Mr Beeston. Even in the middle of all this I have thought often of all the lads we have lost since we started out from England, I am lucky that my best friends have got through. Besides those in the platoon there is Colin Hartley in 'A' Coy★ and young Hoppy who went to the Pioneers. But there are many whom I knew and now their parents must be feeling very acutely at a time like this.

I have hated above all thinking that you might have to suffer in that way, it wasn't so much for myself. We have had our bad times in this war, even our differences, but it has taught me a lot, among other things how lucky I have been to have a home like mine and you for my parents. And so, at this time – I would like to say – thank you for your love, sympathy and understanding at this terrible time.

How long it will be before I see you I don't know – I am hoping they call out teachers soon. But we must wait a little longer – and then I hope home for good with all this past, but not quite forgotten.

All my love to my dear Mother and Dad.

Albert

★Here he is talking about Colin Hartley of A Company, who became his best man, while 'young Hoppy' must have been a friend we have not heard about before, and who was transferred to the Pioneers, a company specialising in light engineering.

My father did keep close contact with Colin Hartley, who a year later was the best man at my parents' wedding. The two old army chums can be seen 30 years later, arms on shoulders on top of Win Hill in the Derbyshire Peak District where my father was then the headmaster at the Hope County Primary School.

Each year in September there is the memorial service to commemorate the Arnhem battle of 1944, to remember the many who lost their lives then. Liberation Day is still celebrated and much effort has gone into ensuring all young Dutch children are aware of the history of those last years of the war and the debt owed to the thousands of young men who died in battle.

My father and Colin (left) while still in the army and (right) 30 years on, reunited in Derbyshire.

ARNHEMS OORLOGSMUSEUM
IndustriePark KLEEFSE WAARD

5e
Polar Bear Mars
zaterdag 13 april 2002

Ontvangst deelnemers v.a. 10 u. op het
IndustriePark Kleefse Waard.
Start van 11 tot 12 uur.

Hierbij informatie en uw deelnemerskaart die op de startpost na betaling geldig gemaakt wordt.

Meerdere kaarten aan de startpost verkrijgbaar. Ook te bestellen door overmaking van € 0,50 voor portikosten (ongeacht het aantal), op Postbanknr. 78 65 356 t.n.v. Polar Bear Mars Arnhem. S.v.p aantal vermelden! Overmaken vóór 1 april a.s.

The Polar Bears will always be remembered.

CHAPTER SIXTEEN

Courtship post-war, May 1945 to April 1946

The final chapter of Sergeant Cartwright's army career

Unfortunately my father's wish to be released and demobilised very quickly, in the hope that qualified teachers would be discharged as a priority, did not happen. But from what he wrote he was not unhappy, and the courtship with the pretty young nurse continued.

My father takes up the story again:

Oddly enough we were returned to Velp on the 17th May, which suited me fine, but eventually moved into Germany where I was stationed at Brilon. There followed some of the happiest days of my life. I was asked to

Sergeant Cartwright at Brilon, Germany, with 'Lofty' and 'Lolly'.

join the Education Corps as sergeant – it was really a con – we all enjoyed it, students as well. There was time for Battalion football matches, visits to Holland. I remember going just before Christmas, laden with cigarettes, which Opa Holland demolished at an alarming rate.

Xmas Greetings 1945

Good wishes home to the family, Christmas 1945.

The 4th Lincolns left Arnhem early in the morning of Wednesday 23 May. The first stage of the journey took them along the familiar road to Velp, and from there within two hours they were across the German border. The countryside looked peaceful enough, but the scenes of devastation and destruction caused by the fighting after the drive by the 2nd Army through to Hamburg and the Baltic were all too evident. They stayed a short while at Glandorf, a small town near Münster, before moving on to Brilon, in central Germany, some 250 kilometres east of Arnhem. My father says little about his duties there, and merely refers to it as the place the Lincolns were sent to, in order to take over the duties of supervision of the camp, a role they were not familiar with. The American forces had been responsible for capturing most of the enemy, but now expected the British Army to take over the job of guarding the temporary resettlement camps. It was a chaotic situation as the camps were occupied by displaced persons of all nationalities – Russians, Poles, Italians and Dutch mainly. Among the photographs kept by my father is one taken of the catering staff at Brilon, and recorded on the back of the photograph are the words 'Mixture of English, Pole and Czech cookery assistants, Brilon, Germany '45'.

During those months in summer 1945, no one knew what to expect about life in the resettlement camps in Holland following the end of hostilities. As those held in the camp were not German prisoners of war, they were allowed outside during the day. However, the night curfew was readily broken, the wires surrounding the camps often cut, and incidents of theft and break-ins frequently reported, sometimes involving the local German population. As my father wrote up, there was cheap availability of cigarettes, with tobacco used as a form of currency. The process of demobilisation had started, although many of the Lincolns must have wondered why it was taking so long. After all, most of the German POWs had been returned home, and although the war with Japan continued, the war being fought by the Lincolns had finished. The Battalion was now regularly publishing its own newspaper, rather splendidly called *The Organ of the 4th Battalion Lincolnshire Regiment*, but sensibly known as the *Lincoln Imp*. It was published as a weekly newspaper and some copies were found among all the Second World War articles my parents had kept. On the front page of the issue of 3 December 1945, it reports on the football match of the Imps vs 1 Corps Troop REME, and the second paragraph reads as follows: *'The Imps asserted their authority right from the start and both Clark (D Coy) and Sgt Cartwright soon tested the visiting goalkeeper.'*

So we have confirmation that Sergeant Cartwright was able play football again, and had retained his skills!

This edition is also a clue to the continuation of my parents' relationship and their courtship, for the lead article on the front page is written by my mother, and the headline reads:

'THE ISLAND AFTER THE CAPITULATION'.

The introduction to the article says *This article was contributed by a Dutch civilian – Miss Nies Rutgers, who works as a nurse in the hospital at Velp – well remembered suburb of Arnhem.* We must assume the guest writer was suggested by my father!

My mother describes in this article the scene the civilian refugees found on their return to the homes they had left on 'The Island', as they made their way along the shell-shattered road from Nijmegen. They were brought in Red Cross lorries from Belgium. Some found only front steps remaining of what had been their home. The once fertile fields were still littered with animal corpses attended by hordes of flies, a grim and sad sight. She describes how the displaced population from other areas tried to enter the Island illegally, how special books were issued to entitle those returning to be supplied with tools, pots, pans and cutlery. Disease was still rife, and Red Cross parcels were still needed to supply food. Work was started to drain and restore the flooded orchards to make the place home again to hundreds of Dutch people.

How the article was researched and written we don't know. Did my mother visit Brilon? I think not. It must have been given to my father to

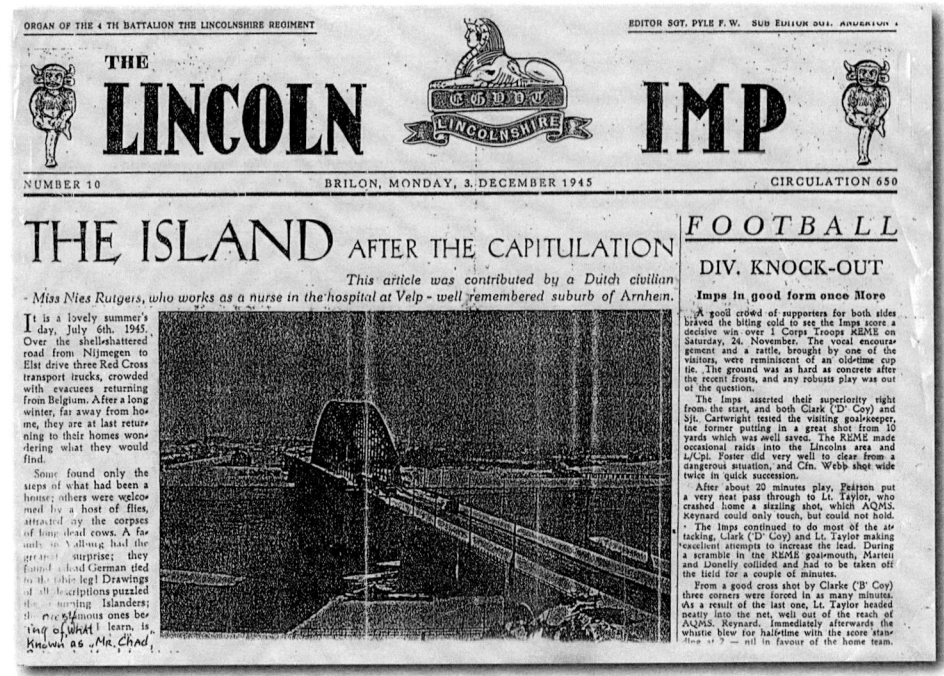

ORGAN OF THE 4 TH BATTALION THE LINCOLNSHIRE REGIMENT · EDITOR SGT. PYLE F. W.   SUB EDITOR SGT. ANDERSON

THE LINCOLN IMP

NUMBER 10 · BRILON, MONDAY, 3 DECEMBER 1945 · CIRCULATION 650

THE ISLAND AFTER THE CAPITULATION

This article was contributed by a Dutch civilian Miss Nies Rutgers, who works as a nurse in the hospital at Velp - well remembered suburb of Arnhem.

It is a lovely summer's day, July 6th. 1945. Over the shell-shattered road from Nijmegen to Elst drive three Red Cross transport trucks, crowded with evacuees returning from Belgium. After a long winter, far away from home, they are at last returning to their homes wondering what they would find.

Some found only the steps of what had been a house; others were welcomed by a host of flies, attracted by the corpses of long dead cows. A far unlikely falling had the grimmest surprise; they found a dead German tied to the bicycle leg! Drawings and descriptions puzzled the returning Islanders; the most famous ones being of what I learn, is known as 'Mr. Chad'.

FOOTBALL

DIV. KNOCK-OUT

Imps in good form once More

A good crowd of supporters for both sides braved the biting cold to see the Imps score a decisive win over 1 Corps Troops REME on Saturday, 24. November. The vocal encouragement and a rattle, brought by one of the visitors, were reminiscent of an old-time cup tie. The ground was as hard as concrete after the recent frosts, and any robusts play was out of the question.

The Imps asserted their superiority right from the start, and both Clark ('D' Coy) and Sjt. Cartwright tested the visiting goalkeeper, the former putting in a great shot from 10 yards which was well saved. The REME made occasional raids into the Lincolns area and L/Cpl. Foster did very well to clear from a dangerous situation, and Cfn. Webb shot wide twice in quick succession.

After about 20 minutes play, Pearson put a very neat pass through to Lt. Taylor, who crashed home a sizzling shot, which AQMS. Keynard could only touch, but could not hold.

The Imps continued to do most of the attacking, Clark ('D' Coy) and Lt. Taylor making excellent attempts to increase the lead. During a scramble in the REME goalmouth, Marten and Donelly collided and had to be taken off the field for a couple of minutes.

From a good cross shot by Clarke ('B' Coy) three corners were forced in as many minutes. As a result of the last one, Lt. Taylor headed neatly into the net, well out of the reach of AQMS. Reynard. Immediately afterwards the whistle blew for half-time with the score standing at 2 — nil in favour of the home team.

My mother visits 'The Island'.

be included in the edition after one of his trips on leave back to Velp. Back in Holland we must assume my mother continued her work at the hospital, although I have found no notes or letters clarifying this. There was communication from my grandfather, Opa Holland, by letter to my father. I was very touched reading these. My parents told my sister that they had taken the decision to remove all the personal letters sent between themselves in their long distance courtship, but these from Opa Holland were left. They clearly show the affection that Opa Holland had for my father, and how he had to come to terms with the fact that they were determined to marry, that my mother would follow my father to England when the time came.

E. RUTGERS   VRIEZENVEEN Sunday Nov. 4th
Dierenarts

Dear Percy,

After having done my usual Sunday afternoon walk – with my darling wife and Wot – also a stick – I have lit one of the cigarettes with one of the matches you left behind last Thursday – wherefore by the way – being a fast smoker. I thanks you very much – and now I want to talk a bit with you.

There are things you better can write rather than say them. Though I perceive, writing, that to write a foreign language is not quite the same as to read it, and is much more difficult! Therefore I want to write it that we, and thereby I mean the whole family, have indeed enjoyed all the leave days, you have thus far spent in our home! We have indeed come to like and trust you my boy! And that is something! For it is not an easy matter for Dutch parents to see their daughter go to a foreign country, be it 'Old England'!

With regards to your sentiments – you and Nies – I could better refer to the words of the famous German poet Schiller:

'Drum prüfe wer sich ewig bindet, Ob sich das Herz zum Herzen findet Der wahn ist kurz, Die Reue ist lang.'

Though you are in Germany I will try to translate it:

'Therefore search, who shall be tied <bound> for eternity If the heart truly finds the other heart For the illusion is short but the repentance is long.'

Enough – you know how we stand! And in case Nies, during her sojourn in the Hague, learns that it is better to marry before going, it will be well! Yet we have to consider the other matter, that of money! Not being what you call a rich man, yet before the war I would have been able to install Nies into her future home. But now it is so, that we cannot dispose of our money, at least only a little. And I fear that little has only a small value in England. Perhaps though, after some years that will alter! Mother calls, supper is ready. So I end. There is no further news. All is well here. Riekje is very much better. The 'ambliae' have got their razor blades and now they don't look dangerous at all.

A firm hand from me, hearty greetings from the whole family,
Yours affect

E. Rutgers

This is of comfort to the family, because we had understood that Opa Holland was opposed to the marriage and would not support it. It was clearly an emotional and complex time, my mother being determined, or even head-strong in love to travel to England to marry her soldier. Opa Holland – a very proud man – must have keenly felt his inability to give more financial support to the marriage.

A second letter was dated 6 December 1945:

E. RUTGERS   VRIEZENVEEN 6th December 1945
Dierenarts

Dear Percy,

I received your letter and I thank you for your honesty! That was not easy for you my boy! Now you must know that when I was your age, I did not have the same strength of faith that I have got now – only a shadow. And most of my friends hold the same reasoning as you do: just live your own life. So I can understand your feelings. But I regret! For you! For life is so much more worth living if you know – by your faith – that you don't have to go alone! And, you know, the only way to get it is – by asking, which we call: praying ! For God is the only one, who can have the mercy to give it! No man, no priest, no church! You shall have to read your Bible – and do it dayly [sic] – asking – for therein is God and Jesus Christ.

Now my boy, I believe, religious thinking as you now do, that a mar-riage in church is not honest, and second is rather impossible for you, for strictly spoken: you cannot say: Yes, on the religious promises the priest asks of you. You cannot do that, even for Nies! Towards God, everyman (and woman) stands for himself.

Now I have thought a lot about you marrying here or in England. And I like it better you and Nies would come back to your original idea – that is to say: Nies, as your fiancée, to your English surroundings. I believe she can stay two months. If you and Nies feelings have not altered then you can marry in your country – the country where you shall both have to live. Is it, at that time impossible for us to attend the marriage, then we shall regret – but it is not so important as Nies, marrying here and not knowing her future surroundings. We will come to you at the first occasion – as soon as possible. That cannot last long, saying how fast the demobilisation is taking place.

And now Percy, I thank you once more for your honesty! Remember: having the Faith or not, are things, which are with God!

Hope to see you on the 21st.

Till then Yours Affectionately

E. Rutgers

Finally, the time had come for my father to be able to return home to England, following the long period of time spent in Germany after the cessation of hostilities. He finishes his written account with only a few words:

Eventually came 'Demob'. I was sad to say goodbye to men I had shared so much with, although I had a provisional arrangement to see Colin. As soon as I was back in England I went to Harwich to meet your mum. And I think you know the story from there.

The campaign fought by the Polar Bears, the 49th Division, from the beaches of Normandy to the liberation of Holland lasted almost a year. In that time they suffered nearly 11,000 casualties, and 1,642 men were killed in action.

I would like to end the story of the 49th Division in the Second World War with two poems. The first one was written by an officer of D Coy

The romance continues.

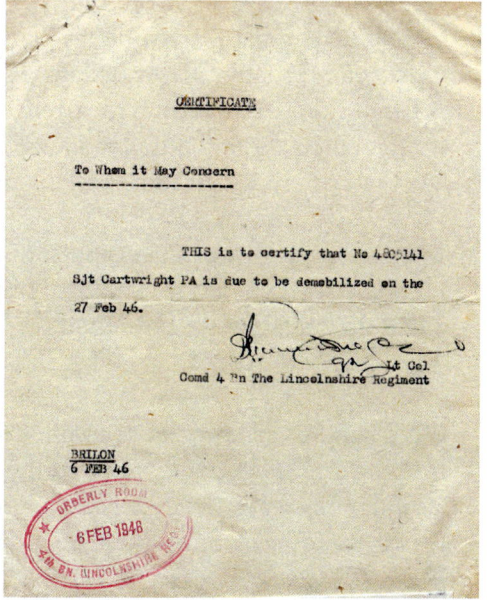

Demob at last.

in 1/4th KOYLI, Captain Lewis Keeble, while the unit was waiting in slit trenches before moving to the start line for the attack on Barbee Farm to the south of Tessel Wood in Normandy where the troops had been held for three weeks. We know this to be the event and period of fighting that left the greatest mark on my father, and which when trying to talk about, he shook his head, reluctant to say much:

'Assembly Area'

Across the pitted freshness of the dewy field
The raucous cordite drifts disturbedly
And hides the frantic-sweating gunners
At their ugly play.

The dawn is shuddering with rutting cries of hate
And far above the black lace trees
The slender moon hangs grey.

I walk apart towards the shattered farm
And look with clear and tender eyes across the past
The frost of autumn and the gas warmed office smell
Far roses of a summer dawn and Sussex bluebells mist.

The barrage gasps and holds its
Fierce inferno blast, a moment's pause in which I hear
Across the fondling waves delight a song of city towers
A faded wisp of melody which tells
Of fragrance and a fragile bridge of love
Made sturdy in a moment's clarity and joy.

Then as the talons of the rising sun search
Lovingly towards the sea the fury breaks again
The soldiers rise with deadened feet and plod across
The sprawling wheat.

Oh death, my friend, my ever-present brother of the dusk
Be kind and if this day you need my company
And draw me ever from the welcome of the sun
Be kind and leave remembrance within my mind.

This second poem was written by Dennis Wilson, a Second World War veteran who was aged 22 when fighting in Normandy. In 2012 he was 91 years old. He wrote his poetry during lulls in the fighting on the front line. He described the horror of war and the life-changing injuries he sustained as a member of the 1st Tyneside Scottish Battalion, the Black Watch. The scenes he witnessed while fighting at Rauray, the area where my father had been fighting 'were so horrific that it pains me to talk about it. I only talk about it to people who were there.' He had ripped out pages from his Field Service Book, and sent them home to his mother during his time in Normandy. The writing was recently rediscovered in his mother's effects, and have been published as a book *Elegy of a Common Soldier*. Wilson has been described as the Wilfred Owen of the Second World War and this is one of his poems:

'Aftermath'

What has war done to the Youth of the World?
It has trained him; mentally to be alert always and to think swiftly;
Physically to endure without food, without sleep, and often without hope.
It has taught him to gaze on the friend who fell beside him in battle,
With less compassion and anger than inward relief:
Relief that the bullet found a heart other than his own;
But relief followed instantly by guilt that will never go away.
It has taught him to think of the enemy framed in the sights of his rifle
Without pity, but only of the kill-or-be killed instincts of the jungle;
And not as a man like himself, with an anxious wife and children
With a small house, and a garden in which to rest on summer ev'nings:
As a man who cares as little for the purpose of the war as he does himself,
And is even now thinking longingly of home …
War has made him incurably restless in a world grown madly impatient;
It has caused him to seek any form of gaudy entertainment promising
   forgetfulness.
It has taught him there is nothing so mean, so lacking-in-glory as war;
And the common peoples of the earth demand only friendship and peace;
But there will always be war, because their Rulers and Mentors lead them
   away from peace. It has taught him that the common peoples must
   unite and destroy the causes of war.
Before their rulers fail again, and they perish with the whole species of
   Humankind.

My father concludes his account, finally, with these words:

> This is the only time I have been through my war years. I came back
> very changed, but in many ways better equipped to begin a career, but at
> which I doubt I would have succeeded without your mother's unfailing
> and cheerful support.

That support is something we knew of. I remember so well his speech to the
whole family at the celebration of their 50th wedding anniversary, when he
started to falter and become emotional as he described their years together
and how he could not have achieved what he wished for without the support
of Nies. A card we discovered among my mother's effects, with the various
photographs, articles and souvenirs, was a picture of Rozendaal, near Velp. It
depicts a large house in the woods and was where they must have walked. I
don't think any of the family had seen it before. My father must have been
talking about his hopes and aspiration for his future and his career, for as we
can see on the next page on the back my mother had written:

Rozendaal, School en Onderwijzerswoning

Do you remember we often walked along this house, it's the house of the head-schoolmaster, on the background is the school. Can't you become such a head-school master?

My father's last visit to Velp.

Yes – as my father said – with his wife's unfailing support he did have a successful teaching career, finishing indeed as a headmaster (but not living in such a house!).

As far as it is possible to tell, the last visit to Velp must have been that February, and almost immediately he will have travelled to England, leaving his future bride to follow him.

CHAPTER SEVENTEEN

Epilogue – marriage, spring 1946

Spring 1946 and marriage

During the time that my father was at Brilon, in Germany, the romance did not falter – as he said in his account he and my mother were in constant touch by letters or visits. After my father's 'demob', he travelled back to England and plans were made for my mother to join him.

But before that, he had to obtain the Army's permission to marry a Dutch civilian.

My mother travelled from the Hook of Holland to the port of Harwich, on the east coast of England, in early 1946, in preparation for her new life

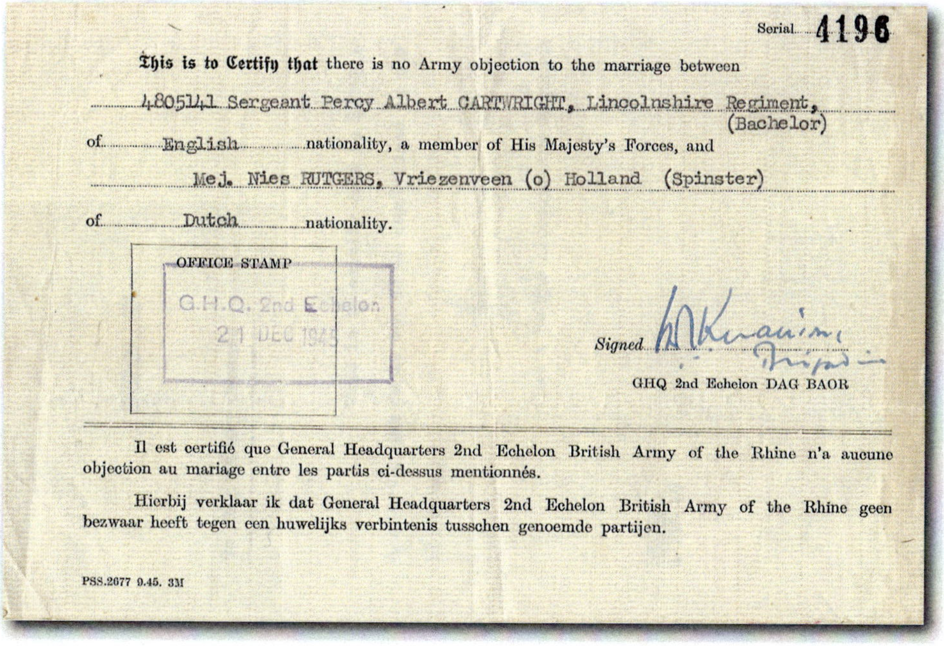

Serial 4196

This is to Certify that there is no Army objection to the marriage between

480541 Sergeant Percy Albert CARTWRIGHT, Lincolnshire Regiment,
(Bachelor)

of English nationality, a member of His Majesty's Forces, and

Mej. Nies RUTGERS, Vriezenveen (o) Holland (Spinster)

of Dutch nationality.

OFFICE STAMP

G.H.Q. 2nd Echelon

21 DEC 1945

Signed ....

GHQ 2nd Echelon DAG BAOR

Il est certifié que General Headquarters 2nd Echelon British Army of the Rhine n'a aucune objection au mariage entre les partis ci-dessus mentionnés.

Hierbij verklaar ik dat General Headquarters 2nd Echelon British Army of the Rhine geen bezwaar heeft tegen een huwelijks verbintenis tusschen genoemde partijen.

PSS.2677 9.45. 33I

Permission to marry granted.

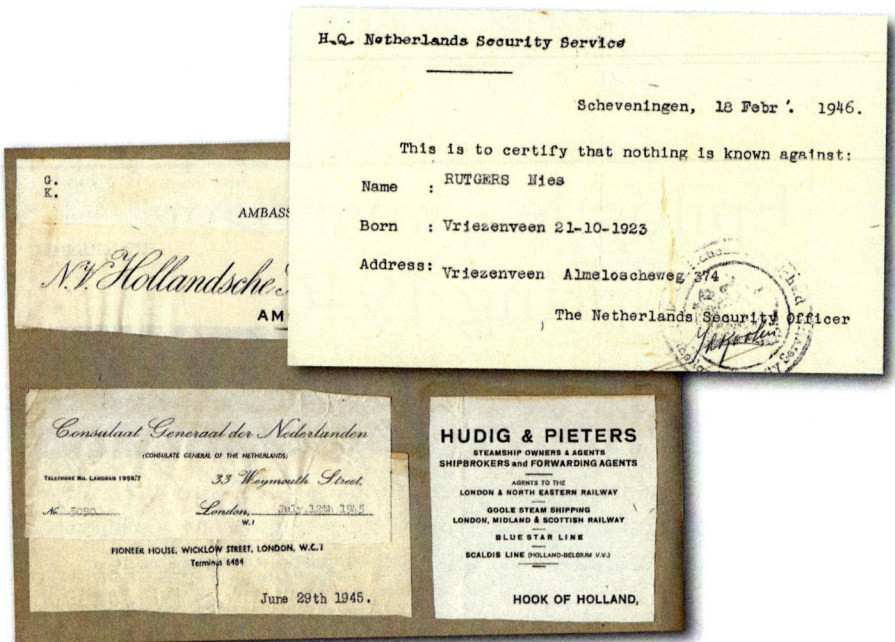

The journey to England.

in England. The date of her ticket and travel was 9 March, the date of my father's birthday!

Before leaving the hospital in January 1946, she obtained a certificate of her nursing qualification and experience – the wording of which must be one of the most understated references it is possible to see!

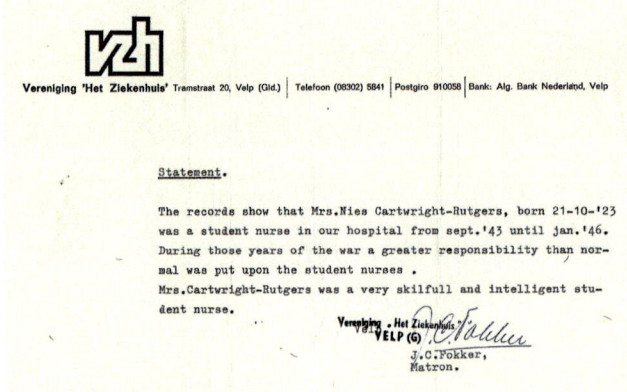

The nursing certificate confirmation.

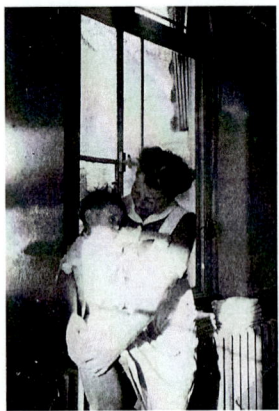

The young nurse cradles a sick child.

We have only one photograph of her in the hospital during those war years – a poignant one of her holding a sick child.

My cousin Nieska told me that her father Johannes, my mother's uncle, was so concerned about her travelling to England with so little money that he gave her £10, a very large sum at the time. A story we all knew was that when my mother arrived at Harwich, after the journey from Holland by boat, my father was not there to meet her, having been delayed in the unpredictable transport situation of the immediate post-war years. When asked by a porter how she could be helped, she said she was waiting for her fiancé, an English soldier, to meet her as planned. The porter must have been thinking 'another young lady who will be upset and heartbroken'. However, my father rushed up along the platform very soon after and found her, the porter having disappeared taking

The happy couple leave the church after their wedding.

the 'tip' of a pound that my mother had given him, not realising the true value of the currency at the time. They were married on 5 April 5 1946. My mother's parents in Holland could not attend, as had been anticipated from the letters that her father wrote to my father, so instead she was given away by Uncle Jack Owens, the husband of Cissy, my father's elder sister.

They spent their honeymoon in Devon and the photographs show them on the beach with my father recording that mum swam, which must have been somewhat chilly in April! The receipts from the small hotel and bed and breakfast accommodation they stayed in were probably typical of the type of honeymoon that could be afforded at those times.

Honeymoon hotel.

Relaxing in the April sunshine – what a contrast to the previous year.

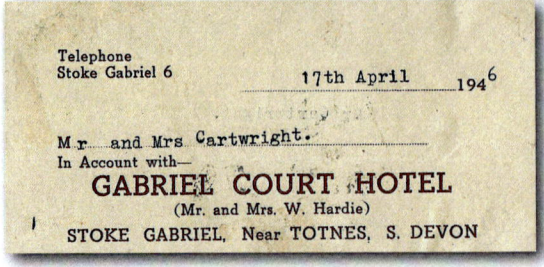

Mr and Mrs Cartwright move to new quarters.

CHAPTER EIGHTEEN

The final days, 2012

My father was over 90 years old before he became increasingly frail, troubled with horrible eczema. Following a fall, he was finally admitted with renal failure to the general hospital in Hereford. Before the ambulance came to take him in, my sister Annemarie described how my mother had struggled up to his bedroom on the stair lift to share a few special minutes alone with him, knowing as they both did that the end of his life, and their life together, was nearly over. He died two days later on 27 February 2012. I knew when I saw him in hospital the evening before he died that he would not survive for long, and from the last conversation we had I remember two things. He was very tired, but conscious, when he asked:

'is your mother OK?'

and then said:

'ask them to turn that noisy bloody thing off.'

It was the beep-beep from the IV infusion to which he had been connected, but soon to be disconnected. He died peacefully the following morning with the family at his bedside.

For my father, there were highs and lows in his successful teaching career. He would have been very relieved to obtain his first post-war teaching post in May 1946, at Stavely, not far from Whitwell. After 11 years came his first post as a headteacher, in the small village primary school at Hope, deep in the heart of the beautiful Peak District of Derbyshire. I know he was happy at Leominster – in his final post as the headmaster in the town primary school – although he never forgot his roots. We talked of the mining industry, and how his home village of Whitwell had changed. He accepted that the coal mine there had now become uneconomical and would have to close,

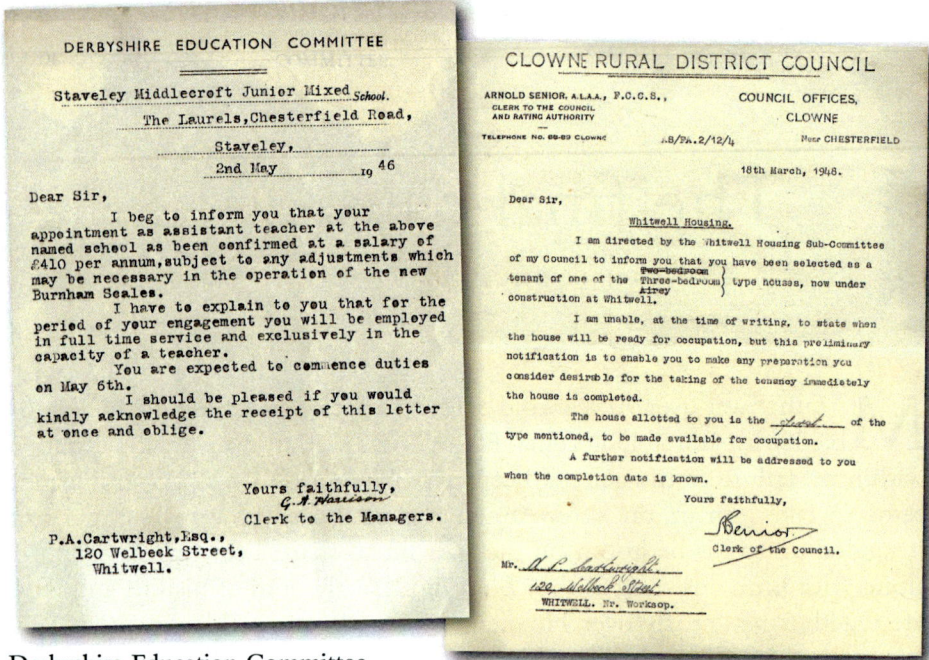

DERBYSHIRE EDUCATION COMMITTEE

Staveley Middlecroft Junior Mixed School.

The Laurels,Chesterfield Road,

Staveley,

2nd May   19 46

Dear Sir,

I beg to inform you that your appointment as assistant teacher at the above named school as been confirmed at a salary of £410 per annum,subject to any adjustments which may be necessary in the operation of the new Burnham Scales.

I have to explain to you that for the period of your engagement you will be employed in full time service and exclusively in the capacity of a teacher.

You are expected to commence duties on May 6th.

I should be pleased if you would kindly acknowledge the receipt of this letter at once and oblige.

Yours faithfully,

G.A.Harrison

Clerk to the Managers.

P.A.Cartwright,Esq.,
120 Welbeck Street,
Whitwell.

CLOWNE RURAL DISTRICT COUNCIL

ARNOLD SENIOR, A.L.A.A., F.C.C.S.,   COUNCIL OFFICES,
CLERK TO THE COUNCIL
AND RATING AUTHORITY   CLOWNE

TELEPHONE No. 88-89 CLOWNE   AB/PA.2/12/4   Near CHESTERFIELD

18th March, 1948.

Dear Sir,

Whitwell Housing.

I am directed by the Whitwell Housing Sub-Committee of my Council to inform you that you have been selected as a tenant of one of the Three-bedroom type houses, now under construction at Whitwell.

I am unable, at the time of writing, to state when the house will be ready for occupation, but this preliminary notification is to enable you to make any preparation you consider desirable for the taking of the tenancy immediately the house is completed.

The house allotted to you is the _____ of the type mentioned, to be made available for occupation.

A further notification will be addressed to you when the completion date is known.

Yours faithfully,

Senior

Clerk of the Council.

Mr. A.P. Cartwright
120 Welbeck Street
WHITWELL. Nr. Worksop.

Derbyshire Education Committee
offers my father the job.   Their own home at last.

but not in the way that the Thatcher government did it. Despite the trauma and horror of his wartime experiences, he did support the Falklands War, or certainly the premise that a country could not be invaded without any consequence.

Together with my mother they were simultaneously presidents of the local Rotary Club and Inner Wheel Society. He retired at the age of 60, enjoyed a game of snooker and golf, and of course music – playing his violin in the Hereford Orchestra. Few retiring headmasters have their work recognised in a personal letter by the constituency MP, but he did, by Peter Temple Morris, the sitting Liberal Democrat constituency MP and a politician he respected.

My mother had some difficult early days after coming to England. It would not have been easy living with Sid and Annie, her parents-in-law, and she was thrilled after many months to be offered council accommodation, in Whitwell, to see us through our early family life before the moves made as my father changed schools and furthered his teaching career.

In those early days of family life in England, it had to be explained to some in the village that she was Dutch not German! She tried to keep us aware of our Dutch heritage; there were, of course, trips to Holland – rare, but always a big event. I remember a taxi being booked to take us to Sheffield to catch the

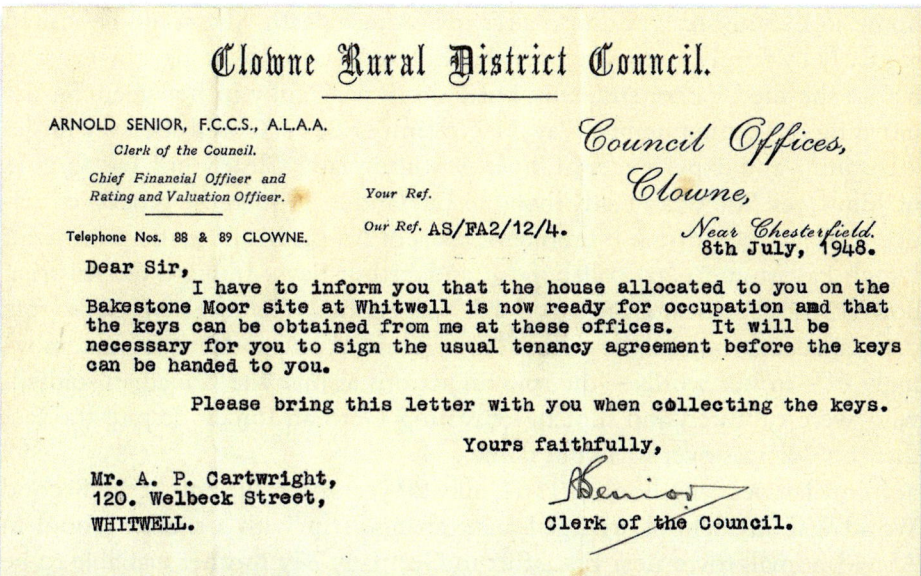

Clowne Rural District Council.

ARNOLD SENIOR, F.C.C.S., A.L.A.A.
Clerk of the Council.

*Chief Financial Officer and
Rating and Valuation Officer.*

Your Ref.

Council Offices,
Clowne,

Telephone Nos. 88 & 89 CLOWNE.

Our Ref. AS/FA2/12/4.

Near Chesterfield.
8th July, 1948.

Dear Sir,
            I have to inform you that the house allocated to you on the
Bakestone Moor site at Whitwell is now ready for occupation and that
the keys can be obtained from me at these offices.   It will be
necessary for you to sign the usual tenancy agreement before the keys
can be handed to you.

            Please bring this letter with you when collecting the keys.

                        Yours faithfully,

Mr. A. P. Cartwright,
120. Welbeck Street,
WHITWELL.

                        Clerk of the Council.

The move is imminent.

train to Hull, for the ferry to the Hook of Holland. So exciting for us but with tears on arrival, seeing her parents and the Dutch family gathered together.

Always in our early days as children we had a small feast on 5 December, 'Sinterklaas Day' in Holland, which is when the Dutch start to celebrate Christmas. There were special treats of goodies brought back from Holland, such as Muisjes (tiny pieces of chocolate similar to mouse droppings!), Appelstroop (lovely concentrated Apple syrup) and of course 'Pannekoeken' on Shrove Tuesday in February. A further treat was to come, when Albert Heijn, the grandson of the founder of the eponymous Dutch supermarket chain, opened a branch of the shop in Hereford. A trip to the 'De Koffie Pot', on the left bank of the river, a development to which Heijn had contributed considerable financial support, was a great pleasure, as all the old favourites such as authentic Gouda cheese could be obtained more easily.

My mother retained her interest in medicine. Her Dutch nursing qualification enabled her to work as a State Enrolled Nurse in the health service but she was capable of much more and it is sad that her ambition could never be realised. She was a gifted linguist and taught German language at evening class at the local secondary school and decided to take English Language at GCE, obtaining a Grade 1 pass – much higher than her children achieved!

The final weeks were difficult for her and as she became more troubled by heart failure and a poor short-term memory she moved into the BUPA care home in Leominster very soon after my father's death. She could be visited regularly by family, and I was only thankful to be able to see her the evening before she died, rather suddenly, but I think peacefully in her sleep, on the morning of Remembrance Day, 11 November 2012. Could she ever forget the trauma and experiences of those wartime years? Clearly not, but forgive, or adjust, yes. She was already living in England in 1946 as the process of justice took place with the Nuremberg trials of Anton Mussert, the prominent Dutch Fascist and Nazi collaborator and Arthur Seyss-Inquart, the Austrian born former Reichskommissar of the Netherlands. She never forgot the role the Canadians took in the liberation of Arnhem and spoke sadly and movingly of – in her words – 'the spiteful actions against the Canadian soldiers, who were captured and shot by retreating German forces, despite the fact that the war was over in all but name'.

In my last year at school, in 1964, only 20 years after the end of the Second World War, my school arranged an exchange trip with a similar school in Alsfeld, a small town near Frankfurt in Germany. My mother was able to be generous and my exchange student was a polite boy, whom we liked, but I never told her that on the repeat exchange when I went to Germany, I saw

a picture of his father, on the drawer or mantelpiece, proudly wearing a black uniform and cap. I have to assume he had been a member of the Nazi SS.

I was born nine months after my parents took their honeymoon in Devon and the staff at the hospital in Holland did not forget their colleague who had been with them during those difficult times.

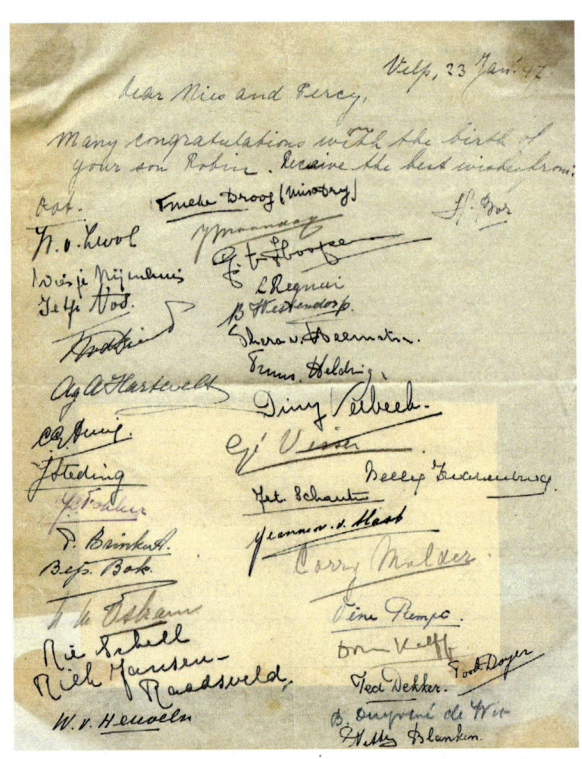

The staff at Velp send congratulations after my birth.

And wedding celebrations became a Diamond 60th. Cutting the cake.

Presidents of the Rotary Club.

Leominster Priory Church

In Loving Memory
of
Nies Cartwright
Who passed away on 11th November 2012
Aged 89 years

Leominster Priory Church

In Loving Memory
of
Percy Albert Cartwright
Who passed away on
27th February 2012
Aged 94 years

Thursday 8th March 2012 at 12.30 pm
followed by cremation

Sharing the sunshine in the beautiful Herefordshire countryside.

My parents went on to have 5 children, 12 grandchildren, and had 4 great-grandchildren by the time they both died.

And their funeral services were celebrations of an undiminished love, lives fully lived, a gathering of family members from all over England and Holland. The service sheets show the daffodils of March and April – 'their time of year' – and of course the Dutch tulips.

Bibliography and sources

Arthur, Max and the Imperial War Museum *Forgotten Voices of the Second World War*. Ebury Press, 2004.

Barker, General E. H. *Diary*.

Belcham, Major-General David *Victory in Normandy*. Clarke Irwin, 1978.

Benson, John *Saturday Night Soldiers: The 4th Lincolns in World War 2*. Richard Kay Publications, 2002.

Benson, John *The Lincolns*. Richard Kay Publications, 2003.

Bryson, Bill *Notes from a Small Island*. Harper Collins Publishers, 1995.

Committee de 4 Mei Velp. *Herinneringen aan de Bevrijding van Velp, 16 April 1945*. Stichting Velp voor Orange, 2006.

Cross, James *Old Whitwell*. Whittington Moor Printing Ltd 1989.

Delaforce, Patrick *The Polar Bears: Monty's Left Flank*. Chancellor Press, 1989.

Evans, David *A Guide to the Beaches and Battlefields of Normandy*. Michael Joseph Ltd, 1994.

Frank, Otto *The Diary of a Young Girl*. Contact Publishing Amsterdam, 1947.

Gies, Miep and Gold, Alison Leslie *Anne Frank Remembered*. Simon and Schuster, 1987.

Goodell, Jane *They Sent me to Iceland*. Facsimile Publishing, 2015.

Hagen, Louis *Arnhem Lift: A Fighting Glider Pilot Remembers*. Severn House Publishers Ltd, 1977.

Hastings, Max *All Hell Let Loose: The World at War 1939–1945*. Harper Press, 2011.

Hesse, Monica *Girl in the Blue Coat*. Macmillian Books, 2016.

Huyskamp, Ruud *Desperate Times, Desperate Measures: German Oppression, Dutch Resistance, and the Tragedy at De Woeste Hoeve*. PhD thesis, University of British Columbia, Okanagan, 2011.

Jackson, Mick *The Underground Man*. Picador, 1997.

Jansen, S. *Velp en de Oorlog 1940–1945*. Stichting Velp voor Orange, 2006.

Jarmain, John 'At a War Grave'. Available at www.allpoetry.com

Jarmain, John 'Flowers in the Minefields: El Alamein to St Honorine'. Flagon Press, 2012.

Joseph, Fiona *Beatrice: The Cadbury Heiress Who Gave Away Her Fortune*. Foxwell Press, 2012.

Montgomery, Field Marshall the Viscount B. *Normandy to the Baltic*. Hutchinson & Co.,1946.

O'Reilly, John P. *156 Parachute Battalion: From Delhi to Arnhem*. Thoroton Publishing Ltd, 2009.

Onderwater, Hans *Operation Manna/Chowhound: The Allied Food Dropping April/May 1945*. Midland Publishing, 1994.

Peet, Mal *Tamar*. Walker Books, 2005.

Phillips, Norman Charles (Canadian-Netherlands Committee) *Holland and the Canadians*. Contact Publishing Group Amsterdam, 1946.

Roseman, Mark *The Villa, The Lake, The Meeting: Wannsee and the Final Solution*. Penguin Books, 2003.

Rossiter, Mike *We Fought at Arnhem*. Bantam Press, an imprint of Transworld Publishers, 2011.

Ryan, Cornelius *A Bridge too Far*. Hamish Hamilton Associates, 1975.

Sebald, W. G. *On the Natural History of Destruction*. Penguin Books, 2004.

Shem-Tov, Tami *Letters from Nowhere*. Dvir Publishing House Ltd, 2007.

Smith, Lyn *Heroes of the Holocaust: Ordinary Britons Who Risked Their Lives to Make a Difference*. Ebury Press, 2013.

Stockum, Hilda van *The Winged Watchman*. Farrar Straus, 1962.

Van der Zee, Henri A. *The Hunger Winter: Occupied Holland 1944–1945*. University of Nebraska Press, 1998.

Verhoeven Paul (Co-writer and Director) *Black Book* (Film) 2006.

Wakefield, John *Dad's War*. Personal publication, 2012.

Wheldon, Sir Huw *Red Berets into Normandy: 6th Airborne Division's Assault into Normandy D Day 1944 (Breydon)*. Jarrold Publishing,1982.

Whiting, Charles *Bounce the Rhine*. Book Club Associates in association with Secker and Warburg Ltd, 1985.

Wilson, Dennis B. *Elegy of a Common Soldier and other Poems*. Kultura Press, 2012.

Wistrich, Robert S. *Hitler and the Holocaust*. A Modern Library Chronicles Book, 2001.

Wolf, Diane *Beyond Anne Frank: Hidden Children and Postwar Families in Holland*. University of California Press, 2007.

Appendices

Appendix 1 – My father's own account

Dear Anne,

You asked me recently if I would write about my experiences in the War. This is something I have never done, & may even have avoided, but since you obviously attached some importance to it I have decided to try & put some memories together. At times in Normandy, it is difficult to remember where you were – or even why – so they are – just memories.

I was in my first teaching post at Swinebrook (Emb. from Whitwell) when called up in Jan. 1940. "Hopty" Bangin, from Wardlcop, was in the same batch & we were still together at the end of the War.

We trained at Lincoln Barracks & in May, went to Hawick, Scotland, to join the 4th Lincolns. 24th June we sailed to Iceland – to Akureyri. Looking back, this was a good

place to me. By Autumn We were   2.
in Nissen huts. As it is practically
in the Arctic circle. it's dark for
virtually 24 hrs. in December, & the
reverse in June. But it's not really
dark, & the Northern lights are
fascinating. It was very healthy (I
never had a cold there!) Akureyri
- 6,000 people - had a small cinema.
& warm, outdoor pool. Training was
all year round - I remember being
lost & walking over a glacier, &
camping out in February. I
played lots of football - & played
violin with the "Northern lights
Dance Band" who actually broadcast
for Reykjavik!
        We returned to U.K. Sept. '42
- night train from Glasgow to
Hereford. There I went to a
Company as Corporal - training
young recruits. This went well for
some months, until I was returned
to ranks for the heinous crime of
coming back late! At this, knowing
my pay was irrelevant as the
Education Authority made up the

balance whatever it was,
I applied to join the Mortar Platoon,
where "Lofty" & other friends were
settled.

Much training followed in
Scotland & Suffolk until we
embarked for France from London.
We landed on D+4 (should have
been D+1). All was quiet, (except for
those on the Carrier which began
to sink, & they had to "swim" for it)
Our first position was in a field;
the routine, as for some 2-3 months,
was to dig your own "slit-trench"
(6' x 3' x 1'6") – after first digging
the large circular pit for the mortar.

Our first action – & one of
the worst, began about 6 a.m., June
25th – the attack on Fontenay. We
reached our position (a large barn
+ orchard) and dug the mortar-
pit, when we were hit by shells,
whining in, & exploding. This –
and being the first time – was

frightening, & went on for ⁴some
20 minutes. I was in the pit with
Sid Hall (still alive - in Doncastle).
A strange quiet then - & we expected
a follow up attack. Nothing. As
we emerged, & took stock, it was
bad. On that day 14 of the Battalion
were killed - 7 were from the Mortar
Platoon. Enough of that.

There followed a period of
moving forward - digging in - firing -
sleeping in slit-trenches, until we
took a position near Caen, in reserve.

From there we moved forward
- comparitively easily, and I saw
the first civilian. As we moved
up the long-sloping field, there
was a small house which had to
be investigated. It was utterly
shattered. Near the fireplace sat
an old lady. She was quite
still - just sat, and stared. There
was nothing we could do - the

5

follow-up troops would take care of her - but, at the time, it all seemed so hopeless. As it did at Breuil-en-Auge, when we took the carrier down to bring out some wounded from the fighting there, & found a young boy of about 11, who again was completely lost. We brought him back to the First-Aid post.

As we moved forward towards Le Havre, I remember the swarms of mosquitoes near Troan - and a broken down house, with a bed still intact, & the feeling of lying on such a thing!

The attack on Le Havre went comparitively easily, thought our infantry had to use flame-throwers. By now we realised that the Mortars were always positioned just behind the front line - an obvious benefit! - though equally - they were a prime target for shelling . (see over)

6

The crossing of Antwerp Turnhout Canal involved much trouble. The mortars were very busy; & for the first - & only time - one shell mis-fired, & plopped gently out of the barrel into the mortar-pit. Three men moved very quickly! It would have been useless, of course, had it exploded. At Poppel, the German counter-attacked, & I remember running for the mortar-pit, & bullets whining through the air. Luckily the Germans were repulsed. I remember a 2 day rest in the grounds of a monastery, & the eerie quietness!

We spent the winter months on the "Island", between Nijmegen & Arnham, mostly living in a deserted farm. Sleeping on a floor was luxury - but lone night guard in a pitch-black barn was not!

7.

That Spring we had what proved to be our last action—the liberation of Arnhem, which, I believe, was where "Skip" was wounded. This was successful; we eventually took up position in the garden of a house which had evidently been a Headquarters for some Nazi command. The walls were decorated with pictures of Adolf etc. Arthur Gill had fun putting a bullet through each one.

We moved forward to an attractive village called Velp, and you know what happened there! Someone came to our billet, & asked if I would come & play the piano—there was a little party involving some nurses. From that point your Mum & I were in constant touch, by letter or visits from Germany.

8.

We had now become used to the excited civilians, or even more so when, whilst we were at Wageningen all Germans in the Netherlands surrendered. Nothing, however, compared to the reception at Utrecht when thousands of Dutch people greeted us as we entered. It was difficult to move through, & all the vehicles were swarming with well-wishers, mostly young girls! — on board.

Oddly enough on 17th May, we returned to Velp, which suited us fine, but eventually moved into Germany, where I was stationed at Brilon. There followed some of the happiest days of my life. I was asked to join the Education Corps as Sgt. It was really a con — we all enjoyed it, "students" as well. There was time for Battalion football matches, & best of all,

9

time to visit Holland. I
remember going just before
Christmas, laden with cigarettes,
which "Opa Holland" demolished
at an alarming rate.

Eventually came "demob".
It was, in a way, sad to say
goodbye to men you'd shared
so much with, (though I had
a provisional arrangement to
see Colin!)

As soon as I was back in
England, I went down to
Harwich to meet your Mum,
and I think you know the
story from then on!

This is the only time I have
ever gone through my Mad years.
I came back very changed, but
in many ways better equipped
to begin a career, but at which
I doubt I would have succeeded
without your Mother's
unfailing & cheerful support,

The Mortar.

The mortar was used to fire shells some 1ft. long x 4" wide.
It was transported, along with shells & 5 men, on a Bren Gun Carrier.
It was placed, if possible, in a large hole, known as the Mortar Pit.
There were 3 parts to it-all heavy. The Base Plate, the Frame, & Barrel.

The Barrel (about 3' long) fitted into the Frame & Base Plate.
The ~~latter had~~ Frame had a mechanism by which the Barrel could be raised or lowered, & swung to L. or R.

When moving into a position the rule was that the Mortar Pit must be dug, & Mortar erected before anything else.

Appendix 2 – the original newspaper articles

NEWS CHRONICLE AND DAILY DISPATCH. MONDAY, SEPTEMBER 17, 1956

The parachutes came drifting down like dandelion clocks through a field of blue and somebody shouted . . .

THEY'RE HERE...

Twelve years ago today the Red Devils, the men of the 1st Airborne Division, parachuted out of the September sky into Arnhem—to fight an epic battle against tremendous odds, to win a place in history. Twelve years ago today Nies Cartwright - Rutgers watched them come floating down . . .

✠

I'D forgotten what peace was like until I went to Velp Hospital, about four miles from Arnhem. But there, in the autumn of 1943, I walked right out of the war—or so I thought.

I remember the first time I saw the hospital on the day matron accepted me as a student nurse.

It was a lovely day. The sun was shining, and the other nurses made me feel immediately at home—or maybe it was the hospital.

From the moment I saw it I loved it. It was as if peace and security and happiness had been mixed with the mortar and the bricks. It was more than a house, it was a home, and the whole staff made the family.

That first day, the nurses who were off duty went mushrooming, and I went with them. When we got back, we fried them and took some for matron, and that surprised me. I never expected a woman who could be so dignified and yet approachable; so efficient and yet so willing to share in any fun.

Her initial interview had been a searching inquiry into my education, family and background, but none of the questions she asked was political. She was looking for a good nurse, and that's what I was hoping to be.

I was thrilled that she had accepted me. Velp had a fine reputation as a teaching hospital.

There was accommodation for about 100 patients, including a number of private cases, and a staff of 70 or 80, and that first day, and for many days after, I thought I was just another nurse in just another hospital.

We worked hard, because matron would settle for nothing less than efficiency, but she had a way of making the simplest, most menial task seem significant and important, and the most inexperienced nurse feel neces-

WOMAN OF ARNHEM
Part One
by NIES
CARTWRIGHT-RUTGERS

NIES CARTWRIGHT-RUTGERS would not like to be called brave.

NOW she is an English housewife, married to a schoolmaster with Robin (10), Jimmy (6) and the twins Barry and Anna-Marie (3) to complete her happiness

THEN she was a nurse in Arnhem, fighting death and the Germans together. Her father and brother were members of the Resistance. Her home had been commandeered by the Germans . . . Here she tells a new and wonderful story of Arnhem.

sary. She was always busy, and she always had time . . .

I realise now that when the youngest nurse on night duty took matron her early morning tea—as she always did—and perched on the edge of the bed to give a report on the

night's happenings, she told matron far more than she thought.

Matron learned as much about the nurse as the nursing, and that was important. It was a matter of life and death that she should know and trust her staff. We were fighting far more than disease in Velp. We were fighting the Germans as well.

I'm not sure when I began to realise that Velp was no ordinary hospital. I think it was when I was washing the medical orderlies' white overalls.

The boys in white

Joop de la Tour and William were not the only boys in white; there were overalls for Tjomme, the local butcher, Jan the baker, and Henk, who was an insurance agent before the Germans came.

"I thought it a little odd, but I was glad of their help and I never asked questions. That was one of the first lessons I learned in Velp.

Then I noticed that the boys used to disappear at night in an ambulance which Wolter, another of the orderlies, had fitted with a home-made generator.

They came back with food and supplies and sometimes stranger cargoes. Sometimes they came back with a patient for the private patients' ward.

Slowly it began to dawn on me that Joop's dark eyes saw far more than the Germans ever knew.

I began to learn a little about some of the private patients, too.

Communist forger

Mr. Bernard, for instance. He was a dramatic-looking man, with a mop of grey hair and burning brown eyes, and his chart didn't make his condition clear. After all, there is no medical name for the sufferings of a Communist under a Nazi regime, and Mr. Bernard had nothing wrong with him that victory wouldn't cure.

His chart said that he was sick, but he was always well enough to forge official papers, provide reliable addresses for escaping prisoners, wrap up food parcels to be smuggled into the prison in the town,

and arrange crazy concerts for us . . .

The Germans would have been interested in those concerts, which were held in the cellars. We made costumes for the nurses' chorus from bandages and surgical gauze, and Mr. Bernard wrote subversive lyrics for us to sing. Mr. Gerritson, another of our private patients, supplied the tunes.

Our star musician

He was our star musician, and the Germans would have been impressed by his violin solos—and by the fact that he was still around . . .

His chart said that he had stomach trouble, and the treatment was mainly isolation. Any contact with the Nazis was liable to be fatal !

Mr. Gerritson was a violinist with the Dutch radio before the war, German by birth, but Dutch by inclination. Unfortunately, he was not naturalised in time.

When he was called up by the Germans he promptly deserted, which is why he arrived at Velp wearing German uniform. The boys buried it in the garden near the mortuary late one night.

That hidden uniform

That hidden uniform explained why Mr. Gerritson's stomach trouble remained interminably acute, and kept him to his room all day.

Slowly I learned about the other side of Velp.

Calmly I was drawn into the other life of the hospital; into the cloak and dagger war. Yet

it was oddly unalarming. Matron and the house surgeon created an aura of calm and we moved in it.

By the time I discovered the false panel in the wall of Nurse Fenna's bedroom, through which the boys were occasionally compelled to disappear at the double, it was no shock to me. No more disturbing than the fact that the bed covers we bought for the beds were not quite the quality or the colours we

could have bought before the war.

We were living in the centre of a cyclone, and it was calm. It was calm that lovely morning in Sept. 1944, when the parachutes came drifting down like dandelion clocks through a field of blue, and somebody shouted: "THEY'RE HERE . . ."

★

TOMORROW :
The battle opens

WOMAN OF ARNHEM — 2

The Battle begins

With her wartime companions Wolter and Dinie, Nies Cartwright-Rutgers (centre) looks out over the Peaceful Rhine and remembers that 12 years ago, this was the battlefield.
Picture by News Chronicle Dispatch chief photographer William Bradley

By NIES CARTWRIGHT-RUTGERS

THE parachutes weaved down to the sunny, dangerous land, and it was Sept. 17, 1944—the first day of the Battle of Arnhem . . .

The throb of the engines made a solid roof of sound beneath the sky, and I stood on the roof of the hospital with the other nurses and waved and cheered the men who couldn't hear us, and wept for the courage and the hope they brought.

But we were nurses, though for those moments we forgot. There were treatments and temperatures and charts to remind us that we were fighting an older war than the one which set the guns barking in the pleasant tree-lined streets of Arnhem a mile or two away.

I wonder now why we weren't more scared.

Perhaps it was that for fear you must have contrast, and we lived with it all the time. We rang St. Elizabeth's Hospital in Arnhem that first day, before the lines went dead. A voice that was strangled with excitement answered the phone, and yelped: "They're in Elizabeth's. They're fighting in the wards . . . It can't be long . . !" And "they" meant the British and "it" meant freedom.

And the girl who took the message went tearing through the wards where the excitement flickered and jumped like a flame, and all we could do was take the temperatures and warm the milk, and wait . . .

That was the first day of Arnhem as I remember it.

If this were my story alone,

This is the story of the Battle of Arnhem and the weeks that followed it—told by an English housewife, then a nurse in a nearby hospital. It is the story of the Red Devils' heroism and the courage of the Dutch people who helped so many to escape.

the five days of the battle would be a confused memory of rumours that drifted and eddied through the hospital like the dust and smoke from a bombed building : of noise and blast that set the bottles dancing on the dispensary shelves ; and of the dogged courage of the patients.

They couldn't move, and yet they could still manage to grin at the incongruity of it all when we gave the order : "Cushions ready . . ." That was the signal which meant the bombs were very close.

THEN— Guns barked in tree-lined streets and sparks showered down like golden rain.

The patients would clap a cushion on their heads and slither down in bed. I remember how proud "one woman was of the splinter she produced from the bedrest near the side of her head.

The rescued

But this is the hospital's story, not just mine. It's the story of William and Joop, Wolter and Jan and all the boys in white. It is also the story of some of the men they saved.

One of those men was Paratrooper Harold Riley, who came from the sedate holiday resort of Lytham St. Annes to Arnhem on a trip that was no

holiday that sunny September day.

He was to become part of the hospital's story, though he didn't know it when he jumped from a Dakota over Arnhem at 500ft.

He remembers the first day of the Battle of Arnhem.

It began with the flight which was too long and too short. Too long to sit in a plane facing another line of men : some of them pretending to sleep ; some trying to crack a joke ; none managing to raise a laugh. And all brave men—afraid. It was too long a flight for that ; too short remembering Arnhem and the job ahead.

The Red Devils swooped

NOW— That pleasant street as it is today—with the new bridge on the right.

into Arnhem and sent their weird wild battle cry of Wahoo-o-Mahomed echoing through the streets.

For Paratrooper Riley and his friends the first day of the Battle of Arnhem began in the sky and ended in the shops and houses which had once been homes, firing with rifles and Sten guns through the windows, and wondering, when they had time to think at all, when the big guns they had been promised would crash out in support.

The refugees

The second day in Velp the refugees came through . . . The Germans evacuated the civilian population of Arnhem, and the hospital was crowded with new casualties.

One of the saddest sights I shall ever see was the old people and the young children helping to push the few possessions they could salvage in invalid chairs, baby carriages, hand carts—anything on wheels. And still in hospital, we could only wait.

In Arnhem on that second day, the sparks from the burning wooden houses showered down like golden rain, and the German tanks

came in. Tirelessly they circled the buildings where the paratroopers fought back with rifles and sten guns and the sort of courage that could manage a laugh.

Our comics slapped a cushion on their heads and hoped the bombs would miss.

The paratrooper in the bombed-out house in Arnhem, picked up a wrecked telephone receiver and dialled Whitehall 1312. "Operator." he said, "get me Mr. Churchill." And above the noise of the guns and the prowling tanks he shouted : "Mr. Churchill, I thought you ought to know. There are some men outside annoying me . . ."

And when he remembers, Paratrooper Riley still has to laugh.

The pattern of the third and fourth days didn't alter. We worked in the hospital and we heard the rumours. That the Red Devils had taken the bridge ; that they had been driven back ; that they were making a last stand in the church ; that they had won.

On the fifth day we knew they had lost . . .

TOMORROW:
No time for despair

WOMAN of ARNHEM—3
THE MAGIC OF ONE RED BERET

NIES CARTRIGHT-RUTGERS

continues her story of Arnhem. It is the story if the Red Devils' heroism and of the courage of the Dutch men and women who daily risked death to help them.

W E went down into Oosterbeek when the battle was over. It was a crazy, dangerous thing to do because it was out of bounds. But it was a crazy world we lived in, and we'd never acquired the habit of observing enemy rules.

We walked through the woods because it was safer that way, and looked down on the deserted town. Red, yellow and green parachutes hung over the battered buildings like the bunting over a carnival town.

Maroon berets were in the dust, so were the crosses which marked where brave men lay.

Torment

It was quiet and still and lost, and then we heard the clump of soldiers' boots as a German patrol came near, and we hid.

I was with Truus, another of the nurses at Velp, and she was trying to find some traces of her mother and father who lived in Oosterbeek.

We found the house. It was split from top to bottom the way you can split a log with an axe. Hundreds of books had been blown down the staircase, and one of them was open at a painting by El Greco. I can see it still, the lovely livid colours and the torment.

In their garden we found the Blue Delph china. I don't know how the cabinet had got into the orchard, but it was there, inches deep in mud with apples rotting round it.

Futility

There was the sickley sweet smell of decay, and the broken china. One cup was still intact, and suddenly the pain was near unbearable. For me, that little china cup held all the futility and all the waste and misery of the war.

We couldn't find Truus's parents, nor anyone who could give us any news. We walked back to the hospital through the woods, and it seemed that the war would never end.

But in the hospital itself, there was no room for misery, and no time for despair. We had more patients than ever before, and more staff. Five doctors from Elizabeth's in Arnhem joined us after the battle, and as soon as they arrived they were absorbed in the odd atmosphere of the hospital. They gave us an ex-

Nies Cartwright-Rutgers, now an English housewife, returns to her native Holland to pay homage to the men who died at Arnhem 12 years ago.

cuse for one of the crazy, incongruous things which were always happening at Velp.

We were all as dangerously involved as we could be ; conditions couldn't have been worse in the hospital—no electricity, no light, apart from the carbide lamps the boys had made, very little fuel and no hot water.

The bombing was incessant, and the boys worked in the wards each day and disappeared at night, and each time they went out they took a chance on their return.

Yet they decided we must have a dinner party.

Beautiful

One of the Arnhem doctors mentioned that he had managed to salvage some very fine wine. "Wonderful," said Joop. "That's just what we need, but we must have a meal to give it proper respect."

The doctor and his wife had brought their two maids with them, and they cooked us the dinner. We had venison out of the bombed cold storage in the town (thanks to the boys !), and it was beautifully cooked and served, though heaven knows how it was done.

The boys each invited a nurse, and we went in to dinner on their arms to dine in the children's ward by candlelight, with music and wine.

It was risky and crazy—but it happened.

Every day, Jan, flaunting the badge of his old regiment in his lapel, used to drift down to the Gestapo headquarters in the town. They thought he was a friend of theirs because he used to take a little sugar or some tea from the hospital supplies.

He would lounge on the desk, talking about this and that, and every day he would memorise a little more of the map on the wall which showed the German fortifications on the Rhine.

When he got back to 'he hospital he drew it neatly for future reference.

At night the boys would disappear. A band of men had come from Arnhem with the doctors. They slept in the children's ward in the day time, and we never asked what they did, nor where they went at night. Then one of them brought us a red beret and a tin hat for a souvenir—the owner had been smuggled to safety across the Rhine.

There was an odd witchcraft in that red beret. I remember we all crowded round just to touch it for luck, as if it were a talisman.

But Velp was a hospital above all things, the underground activities were additional—and incidental. As far as matron and the doctors

were concerned, the patients came first, the other responsibilities they accepted as well. . .

I never remember being miserable in Velp, even when things were grim.

One day in October the English dive-bombed some tanks in the main street of the town. Toot and I were on duty in the children's ward. We just heard one swooping scream and dived under the nearest cots.

When we noticed each other again we were both peering out with a baby under each arm.

The risks

That night the bombing was heavy and the guns were barking, and Mechteld, the laboratory assistant, with staring eyes dashed into my room. "I can't stand it," she screeched, literally tearing her hair. "If it doesn't stop I'll go raving mad . . ."

Two nurses had packed their bags and left the hospital without a word to anyone—because of the bombing —and I thought this was another case.

But it wasn't the war which was worrying Mechteld. It was Mendelsohn's Violin Concerto. Mr. Carritson used to come out at night and practise his violin in the emergency operating theatre under the lab. Apparently he was conscientious.

I laughed. Mendelsohn and Mr. Gerritson had succeeded where air raids, bombs and the Gestapo had failed, and it occurred to me that hysteria induced by the violin was one war risk we never thought we ran.

But there were other risks

TOMORROW

The Gestapo walk in . . .

Woman of Arnhem—4. The day the doctor operated
on a fit man... to save his life!

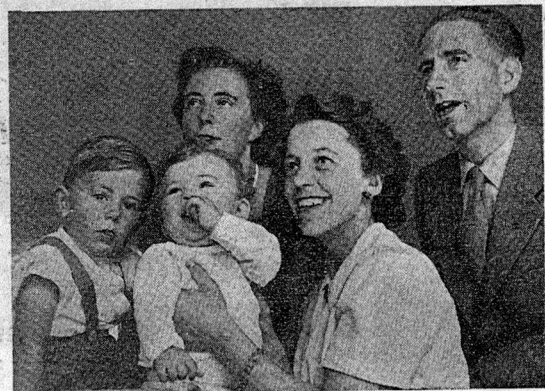

Twelve years ago Wolter hid on the operating table and as Germans searched the doctor took out his perfectly sound appendix. In our picture the author (second from the right) meets Wolter and his family in a happy reunion.

The Gestapo walk in . . .

Nies Cartwright-Rutgers continues her story of Arnhem

WHEN the Germans raided the hospital, the nurse on duty had to think fast to save her life and ours.

The Gestapo were looking for wounded paratroopers. We knew they wouldn't find any in Velp, but there was a lot we didn't want them to discover . . .

An English nurse called Doris Langridge, the adopted daughter of a Dutch family, was on duty at the door. It was her job to take messages, answer the telephone, and keep track of all visitors—including the enemy!

It was an apparently peaceful day in November. For once the guns were fairly quiet and the hospital was calm. It was still calm, in a hectic sort of way, two seconds after Doris saw the patrol and gave the alarm.

Margot had the presence of mind to remember something which might have given us all away. She dashed into the children's ward, swept up the ashtrays with the tablecloth and stuffed the lot in a dirty linen basket. Children don't smoke.

After that she went back to the ward, and wondered what the thermometer would register if she took her own temperature instead of the patients' . . .

I began to realise that anger is stronger than fear. We hated the indignity the search involved and we forgot to be afraid. The Germans seemed to be all over the hospital all at once, and we despised them for being there . . .

But they weren't quite quick enough. The show they missed was like a slapstick comedy, but not funny.

Mr. Bernard shot into bed in the private patients' ward and tried to look as chronic as his chart implied. Mr. Gerritson, Joop and the rest of the wanted men raced straight through the panel in Fenna's bedroom and hid in the hole in the roof.

Scared

One of the doctors actually talked to the Germans, standing with his back to the curtain which covered the panel.

The Germans were too scared to go in the fever ward, and that was lucky for us, because it was there that our radio was hidden.

But Wolter was the one who didn't get away. He became an emergency case. The trolley was wheeled into the shining white operating theatre. The house surgeon and the theatre sister scrubbed up calmly, and Wolter had his appendix out. And the Germans went away.

Long afterwards, remembering it with Fenna, I said I wouldn't have believed that anyone could be as calm and look as cool as the operating surgeon and the nurses who helped him. "Don't you believe it," she said. "He was scared stiff, and so were we . . ."

Trusted

But it didn't show.

It didn't show the day we heard that Pastor Schaars had been sent to Dachau.

To the Germans, he was a dangerous subversive element, but to the people of Velp he was a loved and trusted friend.

He was not actually operating from the hospital, but was the spider in the middle of a web of intrigue. He was the man who knew everything and everybody. And we knew what the Gestapo could do.

We knew, too, that they had long suspected the hospital. They *knew* it was a centre of illegal activity, but they couldn't prove it. They would try hard to persuade the Pastor to talk, and we knew how persuasive they could be.

Those days after the arrest the hospital seemed to die. You could almost touch fear. The arrest was the one thing in everybody's mind, and the one thing that was never spoken. We felt frozen, but not with cold. We found that we wanted to whisper rather than speak aloud.

If there had been any off-duty periods we shouldn't have had anywhere to go. The roads weren't safe, the British were carrying out a non-stop blitz, and the hospital seemed to be balanced on the edge of a world which had turned into a volcano.

Yet we never doubted that it would endure. We never thought about it. It was one of those tremendous things one takes for granted, like the next breath.

We took it for granted that the night the operating theatre was practically disintegrating around us.

It seemed to me that nothing was steady except the House Surgeon's eyes above his mask, and his deft, demanding hands.

The instruments trembled and the walls shook, and the eighteen carbide lamps which gave the only light we had, hissed and flickered round the table.

Many lives were in danger, but one life in that little circle of light could and would be saved.

It was as simple and uncomplicated as that . . .

TOMORROW
Rescue and Romance

Through the wreckage to happiness

WOMAN OF ARNHEM
Nies Cartwright-Rutgers ends her story

Reunited with Margot—"a lively girl with a tremendous zest for life."

THE night Louisa put the bomb under the rose bush I knew nothing on earth could ruffle matron ... It was a noisy night above the ground, and busy down below in the cellars of the hospital which had become the women's and children's ward.

We'd just finished boiling the water for the babies' morning baths. That was a nightly ritual because of the lack of electricity. We used to heat the water over the stove and put it in great pans which were wrapped in blankets so that it would keep moderately warm until the morning. We couldn't afford to keep the stoves alight all night.

The patients were just settling down, and I was planning to do some swotting for the exams which had been put back to December. I was in the throes of blood circulation, chapter three, when a bomb came bouncing down the cellar steps.

I can hear it now—thump ... thump ... It was incredible, unreasonable, but it was there.

Nobody screamed, nobody moved; we just goggled at it, and then Louisa, a big bonnie girl with a slow and ponderous walk, marched across to the bomb, tucked it under her arm like a baby, and went upstairs.

"What have you done with it, nurse?" matron asked.

"I've put it under the rose bush, matron," Louisa said. "The one in the far corner."

Nobody had hysterics, because nobody felt hysterical. That was the effect matron and the house surgeon had.

There were many moments when they must have been afraid, yet nothing was quite so frightening when they were around. You *knew* everything was under control.

Crazy things

We took so many crazy things for granted. I remember Margot disappeared one afternoon and came back bubbling over with excitement. She was Jan's fiancée, a lively, volatile girl with a tremendous zest for life, and she tore back into the hospital chattering about—Blackpool.

Jan had taken her to talk to some English paratroopers who were hiding in a barn. One of them came from Blackpool and Margot's sister had married a Blackpool man so she claimed a sort of proprietary right to the town.

That it was slightly bizarre to be discussing Blackpool in a barn with a man whose life was at stake didn't strike us as particularly odd. That Margot should have this Blackpool fixation was the thing that tickled us.

We told her that any Englishman would be willing to tell a pretty Dutch nurse that he came from Blackpool if he thought it would please her!

Life took on a strange and violent pattern those last weeks before the liberation.

Perhaps it was because there was a pattern that we survived. A hospital imposes its own discipline, and though Velp had lost its gloss it never lost its efficiency.

The women's wards were a series of mattresses crowded on the cellar floor; the lighting was carbide lamps made for us by the boys.

We slept when and where we could. My usual spot was under a bed in the men's ward: "What will you say, nurse," the patient used to ask me with a chuckle, "when I meet you in Arnhem after the war and introduce you as the girl who slept under my bed for weeks?"

The noise of guns and bombs was the background to everything we did.

Silence would have shocked us like an explosion, and somehow, through it all, matron managed to maintain the same serenity and calm which had impressed me that first day I came to Velp.

But then came the most wonderful day of all when the tanks rumbled through Velp, and they were British tanks, and the language that we heard was English, and for us the war was over.

We gave a terrific concert, and a pale little wisp of a girl who used to help the doctor in the town played a supporting role. I didn't know her name then. Now she is called Audrey Hepburn.

The town came back to life. We used to walk through the streets where it was safe to shine a light, and from every battered house came the sound of music and laughter.

And in one deserted house where the french windows had been blown away an English soldier was playing Begin the Beguine. And it is music I shall love all my life, for I married the man who played it.

A paratrooper's postscript

I REMEMBER Margot and Jan. You don't forget people who helped to save your life. I met Jan about five weeks after the Battle of Arnhem. I was riding along the road to Velp on a bicycle—about three sizes too big for me—behind an underground worker, a Dutch policeman. We had just passed several German soldiers, and as one of them moved into the road unslinging his rifle to intercept us, I yawned in his face to allay suspicion. About 50 yards further along, a stern-faced Dutchman stopped the policeman. It looked like trouble. Then the Dutchman, without turning his head, said: "Come on, boys ..." The Dutchman was Jan.

To tell the whole story of those nightmare months after Arnhem would take a book. Enough that I escaped with a friend from the church where the paratroops had made one of their last stands; hid on top of a boiler in a room where the Germans brewed their tea. Escaped from there through the town of Arnhem, being halted five times by Germans on the way. Contacted a Dutchman who dug a hole for us at the back of his garden, and covered us

On a nurse's arm to safety.

with leaves. After 10 days here he took us to a glorified hen coop, where we had to sit crouched all day, and the Germans used the path 10 yards away for testing out machineguns.

Then Jan took us to a house in Velp where we met a pretty girl. That girl was Margot. We did talk about Blackpool, but we also planned our get-away. I walked through the town with Margot on my arm. And I wasn't the first English "boy friend" who might have sent her to a concentration camp, or worse.

★

The underground organisation at Velp provided forged papers, weapons, and finally a passport to freedom. Jan and another of the boys came for us with a Red Cross van and drove us to yet another refuge from where we could make an attempt to escape. They, and others like them, risked their lives and those of their families a hundred times for us and other paratroopers. It was with the help of the Dutch Underground that, after two attempts to escape had failed, we finally drifted in a rowing boat down the River Vaal along the German front line ... to freedom.

I'll never forget them. I am in their debt for ever.

HAROLD RILEY, Lytham St. Annes. Lancs.

The Hepburn story

AUDREY HEPBURN, who was at boarding school in England when World War II broke out, went back to Holland with her mother, the daughter of Baron Arnoud Van Heemstra.

They were in Arnhem when the Germans swarmed into Holland. She saw one of her brothers dragged away by the Nazis for slave labour, and her uncle and one of her cousins were executed.

She first appeared in the hospital at Velp to distribute toys and Christmas parcels for the children from the Red Cross.